From Enclosure to Savanna

From Enclosure to Savanna

Lions in Transition

Sanyub S.

UNIEK ENTERPRISES

CONTENTS

INDEX

Chapter 5 Challenges and Solutions

Chapter 6 The Impact on Conservation

Chapter 7 Looking Ahead

Chapter 8 Conclusion

INTRODUCTION

In the core of the African wild, where the musical beat of nature resounds through the tremendous savannas, a significant change is unfurling. It is an account of versatility, variation, and a guarantee to revamp the story of lions — great dominant hunters that have long caught the human creative mind. From the bounds of fake nooks to the boundless breadth of their normal living space, lions are amidst an excursion that rises above actual limits and represents a change in outlook in the ethos of preservation. This story exemplifies the pith of the progress — From Nook to Savanna — implying a powerful part in the continuous adventure of lion government assistance and protection.

1. **The Thunder that Reverberations:**
   The thunder of a lion, resounding across the savanna, has been an image of force, greatness, and untamed wild for centuries. However, inside the bounds of nooks, that thunder took on an alternate reverberation — a strong reverberation of imprisonment, an indication of obliged opportunity, and a call to rethink our way to deal with the government assistance of these famous animals. As we dive into the intricacies of changing lions from nooks to the far reaching savanna, we leave on an excursion that uncovers the rich embroidery of difficulties, wins, and the multifaceted dance between human stewardship and the intrinsic requirements of these great cats.

2. **The Fenced in area Issue:**
   Limits and Impediments:
   The nook predicament arises as a focal subject in the story of lions. Customary nooks, when thought about fundamental for the security of imperiled species, introduced a two sided deal. While apparently shielding lions, these bound spaces forced impediments on normal ways of behaving, preventing the statement of impulses fashioned through centuries of advancement. The call of the wild, muffled inside the counterfeit limits, reverberated with a supplication

for change.

Mental Effects:

The walled in areas forced mental effects on lions that reached out past actual requirements. Fatigue, stress, and social peculiarities appeared as quiet sobs for a really improving and invigorating climate. Noticing these signs, traditionalists and scientists started to wrestle with the moral ramifications of keeping up with lions in spaces that neglected to reflect the intricacy and variety of their regular natural surroundings.

3. **The Call for Progress:**

Moral Contemplations and Advancement in Hostage The board:

The call for change reverberated in the lobbies of moral contemplations, provoking a development in hostage the board methods of reasoning. Customary zoo models, based on the reason of diversion, confronted a retribution. A change in perspective toward naturalistic conditions, roomy nooks, and an emphasis on the mental prosperity of hostage creatures got forward movement. This undeniable a critical second — an acknowledgment that the moral compass directing hostage the executives required recalibration.

Logical Experiences and Exploration Discoveries:

Logical experiences and exploration discoveries assumed a vital part in molding the call for progress. Concentrates on creature conduct, stress markers, and the natural significance of dominant hunters offered a nuanced comprehension of the many-sided requirements of lions. Moderates and scientists, equipped with observational proof, supported the reason for changing lions to additional indigenous habitats as a way to upgrade their actual wellbeing, mental prosperity, and by and large personal satisfaction.

4. **The Scene of the Savanna:**

The Savanna as a Characteristic Safe house:

The savanna, with its huge fields, acacia-specked scenes, and ensemble of untamed life, arose as the normal shelter for lions. It addresses not only a geological space but rather a powerful environment where the mind boggling dance of hunter and prey, the influence of grasses in the breeze, and the transaction of life's horde structures make an ensemble of unrivaled excellence. The savanna coaxes lions back to their foundations, welcoming them to recover their spot in the perplexing snare of life.

Environmental Congruity and Dominant hunter Elements:

The savanna exemplifies environmental concordance, where lions assume a significant part as dominant hunters. Their presence directs prey populaces, forestalling uncontrolled herbivore development that could prompt environment debasement. The progress to the savanna isn't just about the government assistance of individual lions; it is an essential move in safeguarding the sensitive equilibrium of environments and guaranteeing the flexibility of biodiversity.

5. **The Progress Interaction:**
   Hereditary Contemplations and Protection Rearing:
   The progress interaction envelops complex contemplations, with hereditary variety at its center. Protection rearing projects, directed by logical standards, plan to keep up with hereditary heartiness among hostage populaces. The unpredictable dance of matching lions for rearing, forestalling inbreeding, and decisively overseeing hereditary variety frames a basic part of the change interaction.
   Human-Natural life Conjunction:
   As lions change to the savanna, the story turns towards human-untamed life conjunction. Local area commitment becomes principal, as nearby populaces become stewards of the common scene. Grasping the subtleties of human-lion connections, moderating struggles, and cultivating a feeling of shared liability characterize the progress of the change cycle. The thunder of lions, when a far off and once in a while dreaded sound, changes into a song of concurrence.

6. **Protection Suggestions and Renewed introduction Drives:**
   Connecting Hostage and Wild Populaces:
   Preservation suggestions unfurl in the many-sided dance among hostage and wild lion populaces. Composed hostage lions, brought into the world from moral rearing practices and flourishing in naturalistic conditions, become expected contender for renewed introduction drives. The crossing over of hostage and wild populaces turns into an amicable harmony in the orchestra of lion protection, underlining the interconnectedness of these two domains.
   Renewed introduction Difficulties and Versatile Methodologies:
   Renewed introduction drives deliver a bunch of difficulties and require versatile methodologies. The progressed lions should explore the intricacies of recovering their spot in the wild — figuring out how to chase, lay out regions, and explore the complex social elements of wild prides. Protectionists, outfitted with illustrations gained from past renewed introduction attempts, adjust their procedures to guarantee the fruitful coordination of lions into their local natural surroundings.

7. **The Job of Innovation in Observing and Supporting Lions:**
   Constant Checking and Ecological Experiences:
   The joining of innovation turns into a quiet partner in the change cycle. Continuous observing frameworks, inserted with sensors, cameras, and man-made brainpower, offer experiences into the regular routines of lions.
   From following their developments to evaluating feelings of anxiety and ecological circumstances, innovation turns into an amazing asset in guaranteeing the prosperity of lions as they explore the subtleties of their new, more extensive homes.
   Computer based intelligence Helped Social Investigation and Preservation Training:

Man-made consciousness expands its venture into conduct examination, giving preservationists a more profound comprehension of lion conduct. AI calculations perceive designs, distinguish inconsistencies, and add to the developing assortment of information about untamed life conduct. Besides, innovation turns into a mechanism for protection training, offering virtual encounters that interface worldwide crowds with the predicament of lions and the significance of their preservation.

8. **Examples Gained from Previous mishaps and Disappointments: Comprehensive Navigation and Straightforward Practices:**

The call to change from walled in area to savanna is implanted with illustrations gained from previous slip-ups and disappointments. Comprehensive dynamic cycles, where nearby networks, progressives, and scientists work together, arise as a foundation. Straightforward works on, sharing the two triumphs and difficulties, cultivate a culture of constant improvement and versatile administration — a guarantee to gaining from disappointments as much as praising victories.

All encompassing Biological system The board and Environment Contemplations:

Previous oversights highlight the significance of comprehensive biological system the executives. Protection is definitely not a separated undertaking however a powerful transaction of environmental elements. Environment contemplations, perceiving the effect of a changing environment on lion living spaces, guide protection procedures. The source of inspiration underlines an all encompassing methodology that tends to the underlying drivers of difficulties, from natural surroundings misfortune to environment initiated stressors.

9. **Future Ramifications for Lion Protection In light of Change Achievement:**

Flexibility and Variation:

Looking forward, the progress of the change turns into a harbinger of future ramifications for lion preservation. The versatility and transformation showed by lions notwithstanding progress difficulties become directing reference points. The story reaches out past individual examples of overcoming adversity to illuminate more extensive preservation works on, underscoring the requirement for versatility, inclusivity, and a guarantee to the developing necessities of natural life.

Strengthening of Nearby People group:

Future ramifications spin around the strengthening of neighborhood networks. As lions flourish in their regular environments, the advantages of preservation should reach out to the people who share the scene with these dominant hunters. The source of inspiration envelops drives that engage neighborhood networks financially, socially, and biologically, cultivating a feeling of satisfaction and shared proprietorship in the protection venture.

1. Definition of the Enclosure

The expression "nook" summons a horde of implications, from actual hindrances to figurative limits. In the domain of preservation, zoology, and ecological administration, the meaning of a nook reaches out past a simple actual construction. It epitomizes a mind boggling interchange of environmental, moral, and useful contemplations. In this investigation, we dig into the multi-layered meaning of the walled in area, looking at its authentic advancement, different purposes, and the nuanced job it plays in the preservation and government assistance of different species.

1. **Actual Limits:**
   Zoological Nooks:
   At its center, a nook alludes to an actual space assigned to keep and safeguard living creatures. With regards to zoology, zoological nooks are regions intended to house and show creatures. These can go from extensive living spaces imitating regular habitats to more modest fenced in areas that fill explicit preservation or exploration needs. The size, plan, and highlights of these fenced in areas differ, impacted by variables like the species' regular way of behaving, protection objectives, and moral contemplations.
   Herbal Walled in areas:
   Past the collective of animals, the idea of fenced in areas stretches out to plant domains. Herbal nooks, like greenhouses or controlled plant conditions, give a safeguarded space to the development and investigation of different plant species. These spaces expect to grandstand biodiversity, monitor jeopardized plants, and work with investigation into herbal sciences.
2. **Reason and Capability:**
   Preservation and Insurance:
   Nooks serve an essential job in the preservation and security of species. They go about as safe-havens for jeopardized or weak creatures, giving a controlled climate where the dangers of predation, territory obliteration, or human obstruction are limited. Protection centered fenced in areas frequently coordinate reproducing programs, hereditary administration, and examination drives to add to the conservation of biodiversity.
   Schooling and Exploration:
   Instructive and research-centered nooks capability as living labs. Zoos, aquariums, and greenhouses use walled in areas to work with government funded schooling and logical exploration. Guests gain firsthand encounters with untamed life, encouraging an association with nature and advancing mindfulness about preservation challenges. Specialists, then again, use controlled conditions to direct investigations on creature conduct, physiology, and biology.
   Restoration and Renewed introduction:

A few nooks assume a vital part in the restoration and renewed introduction of untamed life. Untamed life recovery focuses frequently use fenced in areas to give impermanent safe house and care to harmed or stranded creatures. Furthermore, controlled conditions empower a steady renewed introduction process, permitting creatures to reacclimate to their regular environment prior to being delivered.

3. **Moral Contemplations:**

Development in Moral Practices:

The meaning of the nook has developed essentially pair with changing cultural qualities and moral contemplations. Conventional zoos, portrayed by little, desolate walled in areas, have confronted examination for compromising the prosperity of hostage creatures. Accordingly, there has been a change in outlook toward additional moral works on, underscoring extensive, naturalistic nooks that focus on the physical and mental soundness of creatures.

Progressively eliminating Customary Displays:

As moral contemplations gain unmistakable quality, there is a slow getting rid of conventional displays that don't line up with present day principles of creature government assistance. The emphasis is on establishing conditions that imitate the normal living spaces of species, giving open doors to mental excitement, social association, and the declaration of regular ways of behaving. The development in moral practices difficulties the traditional thought of the nook as a simple binding space.

4. **Social and Authentic Setting:**

Authentic Viewpoints:

The authentic setting shapes the meaning of the nook. In prior hundreds of years, walled in areas were related with the nook development in horticulture, where normal terrains were privatized. This verifiable point of view, established in land use and possession, gives knowledge into the shifted understandings of the term. In the preservation domain, the verifiable advancement of fenced in areas reflects changing mentalities toward untamed life and nature.

Social Importance:

The meaning of the fenced in area is likewise impacted by social viewpoints. In certain societies, nooks are essential to strict works on, representing holiness and veneration. In others, they might address an association with the land or act as spaces for mutual exercises. Social subtleties add to the assorted translations and uses of the term.

5. **Difficulties and Reactions:**

Reactions of Control:

Notwithstanding their shifted purposes, walled in areas face reactions, essentially connected with the imprisonment of living creatures. Naysayers contend that even the most all around planned walled in areas can't completely reproduce the opportunity and intricacy of creatures' normal territories. The moral discussion encompassing repression brings up issues about the inborn worth of opportunity for aware creatures.

Adjusting Preservation and Government assistance:

One more test is the fragile harmony between preservation objectives and individual government assistance. While walled in areas add to species safeguarding, concerns emerge about the psychological and actual prosperity of individual creatures. Finding some kind of harmony requires consistent endeavors to further develop walled in area configuration, focus on advancement exercises, and execute moral hostage the executives rehearses.

6. **The Eventual fate of Fenced in areas:**

Developments in Plan:

The eventual fate of nooks is molded by progressing developments in plan and innovation. Progressions in living space configuration, consolidating regular elements, shifted geography, and high level improvement amazing open doors, plan to establish conditions that focus on the prosperity of hostage creatures. Innovation, like computer generated simulation, additionally holds the possibility to improve the instructive parts of fenced in areas.

Preservation in Nature:

As preservation endeavors progressively center around saving species in their normal territories, the job of fenced in areas might develop. The accentuation on in-situ preservation, where endeavors are coordinated toward safeguarding and reestablishing regular natural surroundings, challenges customary thoughts of imprisonment. Nooks might assume a temporary part in preservation, supporting species until they can be once again introduced into nature.

B. Historical context of lions in captivity

The verifiable setting of lions in bondage is a rich embroidery woven through the ages of human progress. From the great zoos of old rulers to the advanced asylums molded by preservation objectives, the bondage of lions mirrors mankind's developing relationship with these superb animals. This investigation dives into the authentic parts that account the imprisonment of lions, following the social, emblematic, and utilitarian jobs they have played in social orders across time.

1. **Lions in Antiquated Civilizations:**
   Imagery and Sovereignty:

In the chronicles of old civilizations, lions held a legendary and representative importance. Worshipped for their solidarity, boldness, and majestic bearing, lions became symbols of force and sovereignty. Mesopotamian lords decorated their royal residences with lion themes, and the powerful lion-headed goddess Sekhmet in Egyptian folklore epitomized both assurance and annihilation.

Catching and exhibiting lions in illustrious zoos served as a showcase of abundance as well as an image of the ruler's association with divine credits.

Gladiatorial Displays in Rome:

The loftiness of lions in bondage arrived at its pinnacle in antiquated Rome. Caught from distant terrains as fascinating images of victory, lions became star attractions in gladiatorial games. The Colosseum saw furious fights among lions and warriors, a scene that mixed diversion, power, and majestic strength. The bondage of lions in this setting rose above simple display; it turned into an instinctive articulation of the Roman hunger for greatness and mastery.

2. **Archaic Zoos and Exoticism:**

Regal Assortments and Colorful Showcases:

During the archaic period, European eminence proceeded with the custom of keeping up with zoological displays that exhibited extraordinary creatures, including lions. These assortments, frequently housed inside palace grounds, were arranged to show the ruler's riches, impact, and common associations. Lions, saw as interesting and intriguing, became living images of a ruler's capacity to order and vanquish far off lands.

The Pinnacle of London Zoo:

Outstanding among these middle age zoos was the Pinnacle of London Zoological garden, laid out in the mid thirteenth 100 years. Lions, alongside different animals, were housed inside the Pinnacle's limits, enrapturing the minds of Londoners and guests the same. The presence of lions in such foundations obscured the lines among the real world and dream, encouraging an interest with the wild and obscure.

3. **Renaissance Courts and Emblematic Purposeful anecdotes:**

Metaphorical Portrayals:

The Renaissance time frame saw a recovery of interest in old style goals and imagery. Lions kept on holding an unmistakable spot in the courts of Europe, as living images as well as subjects of imaginative moral stories. Works of art, models, and embroideries portrayed lions in different emblematic jobs, addressing excellencies like mental fortitude, strength, and grandness. The imprisonment of lions, in this specific circumstance, reached out past the actual nook to a domain of creative and scholarly investigation.

Zoological Nurseries and Illumination:

The later phases of the Renaissance saw the rise of zoological nurseries, antecedents to present day zoos. These foundations intended to give both amusement and instruction. Lions, alongside other fascinating creatures, were shown to satisfy public interest in the regular world. The bondage of lions took on another aspect as these zoological nurseries became vehicles for Edification standards, accentuating the significance of information and reason.

4. **Provincial Undertakings and Major Game Hunting:**
   Frontier Gathering and Magnificent Pride:
   The frontier period saw a time of campaigns and investigation, powered by a longing to gather and feature the fauna and greenery of newfound grounds. Lions, considered prizes of royal may, were caught and moved to Europe for show in zoos or as confidential assortments. The imprisonment of lions became interlaced with ideas of frontier predominance and the presentation of supreme ability.
   Major Game Hunting and Preservation Concerns:
   The late nineteenth and mid twentieth hundreds of years saw a flood in major game hunting, with lions as ideal objectives. This period, set apart by the endeavors of trackers like Theodore Roosevelt and Ernest Hemingway, added to a decrease in lion populaces in nature. Worries about the effect of hunting on lion numbers started to arise, laying the preparation for early preservation endeavors.

5. **Advancement of Current Zoos and Protection Drives:**
   Change of Zoos:
   The twentieth century saw a change in outlook in the way of thinking and plan of zoos. The zoos of the past developed into current zoological parks with an emphasis on training, protection, and moral treatment of creatures. Lions, when simple shows, became representatives for their species, encouraging public mindfulness about the difficulties looked by natural life in nature.
   Protection Reproducing Projects:
   Perceiving the weakness of lions in their normal environments, current zoos started preservation reproducing programs. Hostage populaces were painstakingly figured out how to keep up with hereditary variety, and effective reproducing endeavors added to the protection of undermined lion populaces. Zoos progressively assumed a part in ex-situ protection, planning to make a hereditary supply for potential future renewed introduction endeavors.

6. **Moving Ideal models: Moral Contemplations and Safe-havens:**
   Moral Worries in Customary Zoos:
   The last option a piece of the twentieth century brought uplifted consciousness of moral worries related with keeping enormous hunters, including lions, in conventional zoo settings. Pundits contended that control in little nooks frequently prompted conduct issues, medical conditions, and compromised prosperity. The moral talk provoked a reconsideration of the reason and capability of zoos, pushing them to focus on the psychological and actual strength of hostage creatures.
   Rise of Safe-havens:
   In light of these moral worries, untamed life safe-havens arose as options in contrast to conventional zoos. Safe-havens, frequently settled by protection

associations and creature government assistance advocates, intended to give more naturalistic conditions to saved or resigned creatures, including lions. The center moved from diversion to the prosperity of individual creatures, underlining bigger nooks, negligible human impedance, and a promise to deep rooted care.

7. **Contemporary Difficulties and Future Contemplations:**

Adjusting Protection and Creature Government assistance:

The contemporary setting of lions in bondage is set apart by the continuous test of offsetting preservation objectives with the government assistance of individual creatures. Protection rearing projects keep on adding to worldwide endeavors to safeguard hereditary variety, yet concerns endure about the mental prosperity of lions in imprisonment. Finding some kind of harmony between these double objectives stays a continuous test.

Worldwide Endeavors for In-Situ Preservation:

The 21st century has seen a flood in worldwide endeavors for in-situ preservation. Preservation associations, legislatures, and networks team up to safeguard lion living spaces, moderate human-untamed life struggle, and address the main drivers of populace decline. The spotlight has moved from dependence on hostage populaces to complete techniques that defend lions in their regular habitats.

C. Overview of the transition to a savanna-like environment

The change of lions from customary nooks to a savanna-like climate denotes a critical part in the continuous endeavors to reclassify the guidelines of hostage care and advance the prosperity of these famous hunters. This change, driven by a more profound comprehension of the perplexing requirements of lions and a pledge to moral and preservation disapproved of practices, addresses a change in outlook in the manner in which we approach hostage the executives. This outline investigates the diverse components of the progress cycle, enveloping the reasoning, difficulties, and expected advantages of establishing savanna-like conditions for lions.

1. **Reasoning for Change:**

Moral Contemplations:

The shift towards a savanna-like climate for lions is established in moral contemplations that challenge the conventional model of bondage. Perceiving the restrictions and possible impeding impacts of binding enormous, keen hunters in little nooks, the progress tries to give a more naturalistic and invigorating climate. This lines up with the developing agreement that hostage creatures merit day to day environments that help their physical and mental prosperity.

Conduct Enhancement:

Lions, in the wild, show a scope of mind boggling ways of behaving fundamental for their general wellbeing and imperativeness. The savanna-like climate offers amazing open doors for conduct enhancement, permitting lions to take part in exercises like hunting, investigation, and social connection. This not just addresses fatigue and stress frequently saw in customary nooks yet additionally encourages a more normal articulation of their impulses.

2. **Components of a Savanna-Like Climate:**

Far reaching Scenes:

Integral to the change is the arrangement of far reaching scenes that mirror the open, various territories of a savanna. Huge nooks permit lions to meander, investigate, and lay out regions, working with a more dynamic and regular way of life. These scenes are intended to offer an assortment of vegetation, water highlights, and geological components that imitate the intricacy of their local environments.

Environment Variety:

The savanna is portrayed by its rich biodiversity, and repeating this variety in hostage conditions is foremost. Lions changing to a savanna-like setting benefit from different natural surroundings that incorporate meadows, growth, and water sources.

This variety not just backings a more changed and invigorating climate yet in addition energizes the improvement of a scope of abilities fundamental for their endurance.

3. **Preservation Suggestions:**

Spanning Hostage and Wild Populaces:

The change to a savanna-like climate isn't just about upgrading the prosperity of hostage lions yet additionally holds critical ramifications for preservation. Lions brought up in such conditions might act as likely possibility for renewed introduction drives, overcoming any issues among hostage and wild populaces. This encourages a more comprehensive way to deal with preservation, perceiving the interconnectedness of the two domains.

Instructive Open doors:

Savanna-like conditions in imprisonment become useful assets for training. Guests to zoological parks or safe-havens can observer lions in settings all the more firmly lined up with their regular way of behaving. This firsthand experience cultivates a more profound association between the general population and the preservation message, empowering a feeling of obligation and compassion for the predicament of these dominant hunters in nature.

4. **Challenges in the Change Cycle:**

Space Constraints:

One of the chief provokes in changing lions to a savanna-like climate is the impediment of accessible space. Making broad scenes requires critical land assets, and not all offices might have the ability to give the fundamental space to such conditions. Adjusting the requirement for space with pragmatic contemplations represents a ceaseless test in the progress cycle.

Monetary Limitations:

Carrying out the progress includes significant monetary ventures. The formation of naturalistic conditions, environment variety, and continuous support require assets that might strain the spending plans of certain offices. Raising support endeavors, associations, and imaginative funding models become urgent in conquering monetary limitations and guaranteeing the progress of the change.

5. **Examples of overcoming adversity and Contextual investigations:**
   Al Ain Safari:

The Al Ain Safari in the Unified Bedouin Emirates remains as a praiseworthy instance of fruitful change. The safari park gives immense savanna-like environments to its inhabitant lions, offering a different scene with regular highlights, for example, fake slopes, water bodies, and vegetation. The progress of Al Ain Safari features the positive effect of changing lions to conditions that line up with their normal ways of behaving.

SanWild Natural life Asylum:

In South Africa, the SanWild Untamed life Asylum has been at the very front of making extensive, naturalistic environments for lions safeguarded from different circumstances. The asylum stresses the restoration and renewed introduction of hostage lions, planning to give them conditions that empower physical and mental prosperity. These contextual investigations offer significant experiences into the commonsense viewpoints and advantages of the change.

6. **Mechanical Help in Checking and The executives:**
   Continuous Observing Frameworks:

Innovation assumes a significant part in the effective change to a savanna-like climate. Constant checking frameworks, outfitted with sensors and cameras, permit guardians and scientists to remotely notice lions. These frameworks give experiences into the creatures' way of behaving, wellbeing, and cooperations, working with brief reactions to any difficulties that might emerge during the change interaction.

Artificial intelligence Helped Conduct Investigation:

Man-made brainpower (simulated intelligence) adds to the progress by offering modern apparatuses for social examination. AI calculations can observe designs in lion conduct, helping overseers comprehend and answer the developing necessities of individual creatures. Computer based intelligence applications likewise support continuous examination endeavors, adding to a more profound comprehension of hostage lion conduct and government assistance.

7. **Local area Commitment and Human-Natural life Conjunction:**

Local area Inclusion:

Fruitful changes require local area commitment, especially in districts where offices are arranged. Building nearby help and including networks in the change cycle are fundamental for long haul achievement. Instructive projects, outreach drives, and organizations with neighborhood partners make a common feeling of obligation for the prosperity of lions and add to good connections among offices and their encompassing networks.

Moderating Human-Untamed life Struggle:

Lions changing to savanna-like conditions might be arranged in closeness to human settlements. Viable methodologies for relieving human-untamed life struggle become vital to the progress of the change. This includes executing estimates like secure fencing, local area instruction on conjunction, and the advancement of early advance notice frameworks to forestall clashes and guarantee the wellbeing of the two lions and neighborhood populaces.

D. Significance of the shift for lion welfare and conservation

The shift from customary nooks to savanna-like conditions for hostage lions addresses an extraordinary second in the domains of lion government assistance and protection. Past the actual limits of fenced in areas, this progress holds significant ramifications for the prosperity of individual lions and adds to more extensive protection objectives. This investigation digs into the meaning of this change in outlook, analyzing its effect on lion government assistance, the protection scene, and the fragile harmony between the two.

1. **Propelling Lion Government assistance:**
   Upgraded Conduct Articulation:

   The savanna-like conditions give a material to lions to communicate a more extensive scope of normal ways of behaving. In customary walled in areas, constraints in space and intricacy frequently bring about limited ways of behaving. The shift permits lions to participate in exercises like hunting, regional stamping, and social collaborations, encouraging mental and actual excitement. This, thus, adds to a more improved and satisfying life for hostage lions.

   Diminished Pressure and Weariness:

   The dullness of bound spaces can prompt pressure and weariness in hostage creatures. Savanna-like conditions offer powerful scenes with assorted highlights, diminishing stressors related with constrainment. Lions can investigate various territories, cooperate with natural upgrades, and display a collection of ways of behaving that line up with their impulses. The decrease of pressure and weariness contributes fundamentally to the general government assistance of hostage lions.

2. **Protection Effect:**
   Hereditary Variety and Rearing Achievement:

   The shift to savanna-like conditions is indispensable to protection reproducing programs. Bigger nooks give valuable open doors to normal mating ways of behaving and add to keeping up with hereditary variety inside hostage populaces. Guaranteeing sound rearing practices in these conditions is pivotal for the supported progress of reproducing programs, defending the hereditary strength of hostage lions.

Potential for Renewed introduction Drives:

Lions accustomed to savanna-like conditions might act as contender for renewed introduction drives. The scaffold among hostage and wild populaces turns out to be more unmistakable as lions experience environments that intently look like their normal settings. This potential for renewed introduction lines up with more extensive protection objectives, intending to reinforce wild populaces and reestablish harmony to environments.

3. **Instructive Importance:**

Public Mindfulness and Commitment:

The shift to savanna-like conditions improves the instructive worth of hostage lion offices. Guests can observer lions in settings that reflect their regular way of behaving, cultivating a more profound comprehension of these dominant hunters. Schooling turns into an amazing asset for raising public mindfulness about the difficulties looked by lions in the wild, including environment misfortune, human-natural life struggle, and the significance of protection endeavors.

Cultivating Preservation Backing:

In encountering the greatness of lions in conditions that reverberation their normal natural surroundings, guests are bound to become advocates for preservation. The close to home association manufactured between the general population and these grand animals inside savanna-like settings can convert into expanded help for preservation drives, natural surroundings assurance, and worldwide endeavors to get the eventual fate of lions in nature.

4. **Difficulties and Contemplations:**

Adjusting Government assistance and Protection Objectives:

Finding some kind of harmony between the government assistance of individual lions and more extensive protection objectives represents a continuous test. Guaranteeing that the shift to savanna-like conditions meets the different necessities of hostage lions while contributing genuinely to preservation requires cautious preparation, versatile administration, and a pledge to both momentary government assistance and long haul protection goals.

Tending to Space and Monetary Imperatives:

The production of extensive savanna-like conditions requires critical space and monetary assets. Offices face difficulties in obtaining adequate land and allotting assets for the plan, development, and support of these conditions. Defeating these imperatives requires imaginative arrangements, cooperative endeavors, and an acknowledgment of the drawn out benefits for lion government assistance and preservation.

5. **Mechanical Help and Exploration:**
   Observing and Conduct Exploration:
   Innovation assumes an essential part in supporting the shift by giving devices to constant observing and social exploration. High level observing frameworks furnished with sensors and cameras offer experiences into lion conduct inside these new conditions. Research endeavors add to a more profound comprehension of how lions adjust to the change, illuminating continuous upgrades and refinements in hostage the board rehearses.

   Information Driven Preservation Procedures:
   The mechanical help stretches out past checking to add to information driven protection techniques. AI and man-made reasoning help with examining personal conduct standards, stress markers, and the general prosperity of lions. This information illuminates proof based independent direction, improving the viability of both hostage the executives and more extensive protection drives.

6. **Local area Association and Human-Natural life Concurrence:**

   Building Neighborhood Backing:
   Fruitful advances rely upon building neighborhood support and including networks all the while. Teaching and drawing in nearby populaces make a feeling of shared liability regarding lion government assistance and preservation. Offices should lay out certain associations with networks, tending to worries, and encouraging comprehension to guarantee the achievement and supportability of the shift.

   Moderating Human-Natural life Struggle:
   As lions progress to savanna-like conditions, vicinity to human settlements might build the potential for clashes. Alleviating these contentions requires executing estimates like secure fencing, local area training, and cooperative procedures that guarantee the wellbeing of the two lions and neighborhood populaces. Effectively exploring human-natural life conjunction becomes vital to the general progress of the change.

Chapter 1

The Enclosure Era

The Nook Time remains as a urgent period ever, traversing a few centuries and seeing significant changes in the manner land was possessed, developed, and used. This groundbreaking age, transcendently unfurling in Europe from the late middle age time frame to the nineteenth 100 years, denoted a progress from public and open-field frameworks to private property and encased fields. The effects of this time were diverse, influencing the farming scene as well as friendly, financial, and political designs. This exposition dives into the intricacies of the Nook Time, investigating its starting points, main impetuses, results, and persevering through heritage.

Starting points and Main thrusts:

The underlying foundations of the Walled in area Period can be followed back to middle age Britain, where the open-field framework won. In this agrarian model, towns developed huge mutual fields isolated into strips, with every family holding dispersed strips to guarantee fair admittance to rich and less prolific land. Over the long run, different variables merged to challenge this customary framework.

Populace Development:

One of the essential drivers was the critical populace development during the late archaic period. The flood in populace spurred expanded interest for food, coming down on the current horticultural practices to deliver all the more productively.

Mechanical Headways:

Simultaneously, mechanical headways, for example, the reception of the three-field framework and further developed furrowing methods expanded rural efficiency. This, thus, escalated the interest for bigger, merged plots of land that could be overseen all the more proficiently.

Ascent of Free enterprise:

The rise of private enterprise assumed a vital part in the Nook Time. As business sectors extended, there was a developing accentuation on boosting benefits from horticulture. The open-field framework, with its divided plots and public administration, became seen as wasteful and inconsistent with the benefit driven outlook of the blossoming industrialist economy.

Lawful and Institutional Changes:

Legitimate and institutional changes likewise worked with the shift toward walled in areas. Demonstrations of Parliament, like the Resolution of Merton (1236) and the Rule of Westminster (1285), gave lawful systems to landowners to encase and privatize land. Over the long haul, these official measures turned out to be better towards enormous landholders.

The Nook Cycle:

The course of nook included the combination of dispersed strips into bigger, closed in fields. This progress was not uniform and differed across areas and periods. Nook could be started through a few strategies, including parliamentary demonstrations, individual arrangements, or even through the activities of strong landowners.

Parliamentary Nooks:

Parliamentary nooks were formalized through demonstrations of Parliament. These demonstrations conceded landowners the lawful right to encase normal terrains and rearrange them among individual landholders. While advocates contended that parliamentary fenced in area expanded horticultural effectiveness and efficiency, pundits battled that it excessively helped the well off, prompting the dispossession of more modest landholders and country networks.

Individual Arrangements:

Now and again, walled in area happened through individual arrangements between landowners. These arrangements frequently elaborate pay for those whose grounds were encased, albeit the reasonableness of these courses of action was profoundly factor. The shift towards individual arrangements mirrored the changing influence elements and the rising impact of rich landowners.

Financial Tensions:

Financial tensions assumed a critical part in driving nook at the nearby level. Landowners looked to increment benefits by solidifying and privatizing their possessions. The nook of normal terrains frequently prompted the removal of sharecroppers and the union of smallholdings into bigger, more productive homes.

Results of Fenced in area:

The Walled in area Period achieved significant and enduring changes to the agrarian, social, and financial texture of social orders. While defenders contended that fenced in area would prompt expanded horticultural effectiveness and by and large financial turn of events, the results were complicated and frequently dissimilarly affected various portions of the populace.

Horticultural Change:

Nook on a very basic level changed the horticultural scene. Enormous, combined fields supplanted the conventional open-field framework, prompting expanded specialization, further developed proficiency, and the reception of further developed cultivating strategies. The shift towards encased fields took into account the execution of new techniques, for example, crop pivot, which upgraded soil ripeness and efficiency.

Uprooting and Rustic Turmoil:

In any case, the advantages of walled in area were not equitably dispersed. Numerous little ranchers, particularly sharecroppers, were uprooted from their territories, prompting provincial turmoil and fights. The dispossession of the provincial poor frequently brought about relocation to metropolitan focuses looking for work, adding to the development of industrialization.

Social Disparity:

Nook exacerbated social disparity by gathering landownership in the possession of a couple of well off people. The privatization of normal terrains implied that those without admittance to huge capital were prohibited from the advantages of agrarian upgrades. This broadening abundance hole had extensive ramifications for social security and union.

Urbanization and Industrialization:

The deluge of dislodged provincial populaces into metropolitan regions powered the development of urban communities and the expanding modern transformation. The excess work from the field turned into a basic asset for the growing modern labor force, driving the change of economies from agrarian to modern.

Ecological Effect:

The ecological results of walled in area were additionally striking. While the solidification of fields considered more effective land use, the emphasis on expanding efficiency frequently prompted unreasonable farming practices. The constant quest for benefit in some cases brought about abuse of the land, exhaustion of soil richness, and natural corruption.

Tradition of the Nook Period:

The Nook Time made a permanent imprint on the authentic, social, and monetary scenes, molding the direction of countries and affecting resulting advancements. Understanding the getting through tradition of fenced in area requires looking at its effect on different aspects of society.

Property Privileges and Private enterprise:

The shift from shared landownership to private property freedoms during the Fenced in area Time laid the basis for the advancement of entrepreneur economies. The idea of private property became key to the entrepreneur framework, empowering the collection of riches and the foundation of a market-driven monetary structure.

Rustic Metropolitan Gap:

The country metropolitan relocation set off by nook added to the development of a particular rustic metropolitan gap. As individuals moved from agrarian networks to metropolitan focuses, significant social and social changes resulted. The urbanization pattern put into high gear during this period keeps on forming segment designs and cultural designs.

Modern Insurgency:

The Nook Time assumed a synergist part in the Modern Upheaval. The excess workforce created by country dislodging turned into the labor force for prospering ventures. The change from agrarian to modern economies, portrayed by mechanical developments and urbanization, denoted a turning point in mankind's set of experiences.

Current Rural Practices:

The agrarian changes achieved by walled in area keep on impacting present day cultivating rehearses. While nook at first pointed toward expanding efficiency through union, the automation of farming in the nineteenth and twentieth hundreds of years further upset the area. Today, present day cultivating is described by huge scope, automated tasks that follow their underlying foundations back to the fenced in area development.

Social Imbalance and Land Possession:

The grouping of landownership during the Nook Time laid out examples of social disparity that endure right up 'til now. Differences in land possession keep on molding admittance to assets, financial open doors, and political power. The tradition of fenced in area is obvious in contemporary conversations encompassing area change, property freedoms, and civil rights.

1.1 Evolution of Zoos and Wildlife Enclosures

The historical backdrop of zoos and untamed life nooks is a demonstration of humankind's changing relationship with the regular world. What started as zoos and assortments of colorful creatures for the diversion of sovereignty and the inquisitive public has developed into a perplexing organization of establishments committed to protection, schooling, and moral stewardship. This exposition investigates the complex development of zoos, following their beginnings, the shift towards preservation, the difficulties they face, and the continuous endeavors to find some kind of harmony between safeguarding biodiversity and guaranteeing the government assistance of hostage creatures.

Beginnings of Zoos:

The idea of keeping outlandish creatures traces all the way back to old civilizations. The earliest recorded occasions of creatures being saved for show come from Mesopotamia and antiquated Egypt, where rulers gathered colorful animals as images of force and distinction. These early "zoos" or zoological displays, nonetheless, were more similar to superficial points of interest and did essentially nothing to focus on the prosperity of the creatures.

Archaic Zoos:

In archaic Europe, zoos turned out to be more far reaching, frequently connected with regal courts. These assortments filled in as both diversion and articulations of riches. Notwithstanding, the attention stayed on displaying outlandish creatures as opposed to understanding or really focusing on their requirements.

The Period of Investigation:

The Period of Investigation further filled the interest for fascinating animals, as pioneers brought back examples from newfound grounds. The zoos of this period, like those at Versailles and the Pinnacle of London, were loaded up with creatures brought back from the most distant scopes of the globe.

Progress to Present day Zoos:

The nineteenth century denoted a critical change in the way of thinking behind creature assortments. Zoos started to create some distance from simple show and amusement, perceiving the significance of schooling and protection.

The London Zoo (1828):

The kickoff of the London Zoo in 1828 is many times considered a defining moment. Dissimilar to prior zoos, the London Zoo expected to instruct people in general about creatures and their normal ways of behaving. This shift laid the preparation for the cutting edge zoo, stressing a double mission of preservation and public commitment.

Protection and Logical Concentration:

As logical comprehension of creatures expanded, zoos developed to become habitats for examination and preservation. The job of zoos extended past presentation, with a developing accentuation on reproducing programs, species protection, and logical exploration.

Challenges and Moral Worries:

In spite of the positive development towards preservation, present day zoos face various difficulties and moral worries. Adjusting the government assistance of hostage creatures, the instructive objectives of the organization, and the protection basic has turned into a continuous battle.

Creature Government assistance:

Pundits contend that the control of creatures in zoos innately undermines their prosperity. Worries about restricted space, unnatural conditions, and stress-related ways of behaving have ignited banters about the moral ramifications of keeping creatures in bondage, even in all around planned fenced in areas.

Protection Issues:

While zoos contribute altogether to preservation endeavors, challenges exist. The attention on alluring species frequently eclipses less famous or jeopardized ones. Moreover, questions emerge about the adequacy of hostage rearing projects, the expected effect of renewed introduction endeavors, and the job of zoos in protecting environments.

Instructive Viability:

Zoos plan to instruct people in general about untamed life, yet the adequacy of these endeavors is discussed. Some contend that seeing creatures in bondage cultivates an association with nature and moves protection activity. Others battle that such experiences might convey wrong impressions of untamed life conduct and territories.

Moral Contemplations:

Moral worries stretch out to issues like the obtaining of creatures, the treatment of surplus creatures, and the possible double-dealing of natural life for monetary benefit. Straightforwardness in these issues becomes pivotal for keeping up with public trust.

Development of Walled in areas:

The plan and development of nooks have gone through an extraordinary advancement as zoos endeavor to establish conditions that focus on both creature government assistance and guest experience.

Change from Enclosures to Naturalistic Territories:

Early zoos highlighted little, desolate enclosures that frequently neglected to meet the physiological and social requirements of creatures. The shift towards naturalistic living spaces started in the last 50% of the twentieth hundred years. Zoos perceived the significance of giving creatures space, natural advancement, and open doors for mental excitement.

Enhancement and Conduct The board:

The idea of ecological improvement acquired conspicuousness, zeroing in on furnishing creatures with boosts that energize regular ways of behaving. Fenced in areas developed to incorporate highlights like climbing structures, concealing spots, and intelligent components that advance mental and actual commitment.

Instructive Signage and Understanding:

Zoos have progressively integrated instructive signage and understanding into displays. Rather than simply displaying creatures, shows presently mean to illuminate guests about the species' regular history, protection status, and the difficulties they face in nature.

Reproducing and Renewed introduction Projects:

Nooks assume a vital part in hostage reproducing programs. Zoos have become centers for rearing imperiled species, determined to once again introduce posterity into their normal environments. This approach adds to the conservation of hereditary variety and helps reinforce wild populaces.

Progressing Developments and Future Bearings:

Zoos keep on developing in light of advancing cultural assumptions and preservation needs. A few patterns and drives shape the future direction of zoological organizations.

Innovation Mix:

The mix of innovation, like augmented simulation and live streaming, improves the instructive experience for guests. Virtual stages permit individuals to interface with untamed life without the actual requirements of conventional zoos, encouraging a worldwide comprehension of preservation issues.

Coordinated effort and Preservation Associations:

Zoos progressively team up with one another and with preservation associations to address worldwide protection challenges. These associations stretch out past boundaries, accentuating the interconnectedness of biological systems and the requirement for aggregate endeavors.

Accentuation on Neighborhood Biodiversity:

There is a developing accentuation on displaying neighborhood biodiversity to bring issues to light about the significance of saving close by biological systems. Zoos assume a part in teaching networks about the one of a kind vegetation in their districts, empowering a feeling of stewardship for neighborhood natural life.

Guest Commitment and Backing:

Zoos perceive the significance of drawing in guests as promoters for protection. Instructive projects, intuitive shows, and resident science drives enable guests to add to natural life protection endeavors and advance supportable practices.

1.2 The role of captivity in lion conservation

Lions, once broadly disseminated across Africa and portions of Asia, are currently confronting various dangers that have prompted a huge decrease in their populaces. Preservation endeavors for these superb hunters have turned into a worldwide concern, and the job of imprisonment in lion protection has turned into a subject of both help and examination. This exposition investigates the intricacies encompassing the bondage of lions, inspecting the difficulties, possible advantages, and moral contemplations related with involving hostage conditions as a device for lion preservation.

Challenges Confronting Wild Lion Populaces:

Prior to diving into the job of bondage, it is vital to comprehend the difficulties defying wild lion populaces. A few variables add to the decay of lions in the wild, putting forth preservation attempts basic:

Environment Misfortune:

Lions require huge domains for hunting and endurance. Nonetheless, their natural surroundings are progressively divided and lost to human turn of events, farming, and framework projects. The subsequent territory misfortune compounds human-untamed life struggle as lions draw into nearer vicinity to human settlements.

Human-Untamed life Struggle:

As human populaces grow, clashes among people and lions over space and assets heighten. Animals ravaging by lions frequently prompts retaliatory killings by nearby networks, further undermining lion populaces.

Poaching and Unlawful Untamed life Exchange:

Poaching for lion parts, like bones and skins, as well as the unlawful exchange live fledglings, represents a critical danger to wild lion populaces. Interest for these things is driven by social convictions, prize hunting, and the extraordinary pet exchange.

Infection Flare-ups:

Lions are defenseless to illnesses that can obliterate populaces, like canine sickness and cow-like tuberculosis. The spread of sicknesses is exacerbated by human exercises and the vicinity of homegrown creatures to untamed life.

Environmental Change:

Environmental change can possibly modify biological systems and upset prey-hunter connections. Lions might confront moves in adjusting to changing natural circumstances, influencing their endurance.

The Job of Imprisonment in Lion Protection:

Hostage conditions, including zoos, asylums, and rearing offices, have become basic parts of lion preservation methodologies. The job of bondage envelops different exercises pointed toward safeguarding the species and tending to the difficulties looked by wild populaces.

Protection Rearing Projects:

Hostage rearing projects assume a basic part in keeping up with hereditary variety and forestalling the deficiency of novel genealogies. These projects frequently include painstakingly oversaw rearing to guarantee the wellbeing and reasonability of hostage lion populaces.

Schooling and Mindfulness:

Hostage lions in very much oversaw offices add to state funded training and mindfulness about the predicament of lions in nature. Zoos and asylums give chances to individuals to find out about the significance of preservation, the dangers confronting lions, and the job people can play in protection endeavors.

Research Open doors:

Hostage conditions give controlled settings to logical exploration on lion conduct, multiplication, and wellbeing. Concentrating on hostage lions can yield significant bits of knowledge that might illuminate protection procedures for wild populaces.

Renewed introduction Projects:

A few hostage lions are possibility for renewed introduction into nature. Renewed introduction programs intend to support wild populaces by delivering hostage conceived people into reasonable environments, adding to the reclamation of natural equilibrium.

Emergency Reaction and Recovery:

Hostage offices, especially safe-havens, frequently assume an essential part in giving crisis care and restoration to lions protected from critical circumstances, like unlawful dealing or harmful imprisonment. These offices offer another opportunity for lions to carry on with a more normal life.

Challenges Related with Imprisonment:

While the job of imprisonment in lion preservation is diverse, it isn't without challenges and moral contemplations. Tending to these worries is fundamental for guaranteeing the prosperity of individual lions and the adequacy of preservation endeavors:

Moral Contemplations:

The moral quandary of keeping enormous hunters in imprisonment spins around inquiries of creature government assistance, regular way of behaving, and the effect of constrainment on physical and mental wellbeing. Pundits contend that the inborn idea of lions, which require immense domains and complex social designs, can't be enough repeated in bondage.

Hereditary Variety and Inbreeding:

While hostage rearing projects expect to keep up with hereditary variety, worries about inbreeding and the possible loss of wild qualities endure. The drawn out soundness of hostage populaces depends on cautious hereditary administration to forestall pernicious impacts.

Monetary Interests and Double-dealing:

The business parts of imprisonment, including the travel industry, prize hunting, and the colorful pet exchange, can prompt the abuse of lions for monetary benefit. Untrustworthy practices, like canned hunting and flighty reproducing, sabotage certifiable preservation targets.

Government assistance Difficulties:

Guaranteeing the government assistance of hostage lions is a considerable test. Walled in areas should be intended to meet the physical and mental requirements of the creatures, giving adequate room, advancement, and social communications. Insufficient circumstances can prompt pressure, stereotypic ways of behaving, and compromised wellbeing.

Adequacy of Renewed introduction:

Once again introducing hostage conceived lions into the wild represents various difficulties. Achievement relies upon variables, for example, the sufficiency of pre-discharge preparing, the accessibility of appropriate living spaces, and the capacity of delivered people to adjust to nature.

Moral Contemplations in Hostage Lion The board:

Exploring the moral contemplations related with bondage requires cautious thought of the government assistance of individual lions and the more extensive preservation objectives. A few standards guide moral hostage lion the executives:

Empathetic Treatment and Government assistance Guidelines:

Hostage offices should focus on the prosperity of lions, guaranteeing that walled in areas meet or surpass laid out government assistance guidelines. Giving sufficient room, improvement, and veterinary consideration is fundamental for advancing the physical and mental wellbeing of the creatures.

Straightforwardness and Responsibility:

Zoos, safe-havens, and rearing offices should work straightforwardly and be responsible for their activities. Open correspondence about preservation objectives, rearing practices, and the treatment of individual lions cultivates trust among general society and protection partners.

Dependable Reproducing Practices:

Hostage rearing projects ought to stick to dependable practices to stay away from inbreeding and keep up with hereditary variety. Reproducing ought to line up with protection objectives, and surplus creatures shouldn't add to issues, for example, overpopulation or unscrupulous practices like canned hunting.

Schooling and Preservation Informing:

Hostage offices ought to focus on instruction and preservation informing. Guests ought to leave with a more noteworthy comprehension of the difficulties confronting lions in the wild and a feeling of obligation for their preservation.

Preservation Effect Evaluation:

The preservation adequacy of hostage projects ought to be consistently evaluated. This incorporates assessing the outcome of rearing projects, the effect of renewed introduction endeavors, and the commitment of hostage conditions to worldwide lion protection.

1.3 Challenges and criticisms of keeping lions in enclosures

While the act of keeping lions in fenced in areas has been related with different protection and instructive goals, it isn't without its difficulties and reactions. The bondage of lions raises moral worries, government assistance issues, and inquiries concerning the adequacy of such practices in adding to the drawn out endurance of the species. This article investigates a portion of the huge difficulties and reactions related with keeping lions in nooks.

Restricted Space and Normal Way of behaving:

One of the essential reactions of keeping lions in walled in areas is the constraint on space, thwarting the declaration of their normal ways of behaving. In the wild, lions wander immense domains, take part in complex social designs, and display a scope of ways of behaving fundamental for their physical and mental prosperity. Nooks, even those planned with improvement highlights, frequently miss the mark in giving the space and variety required for a full articulation of normal ways of behaving.

Creature Government assistance Concerns:

The government assistance of lions in bondage is a basic concern. Nooks may not generally meet the physical and mental requirements of these dominant hunters. Deficient space, absence of natural advancement, and restricted open doors for hunting and social cooperations can prompt pressure, weariness, and the improvement of stereotypic ways of behaving — redundant, purposeless activities demonstrative of mental trouble.

Hereditary Variety and Inbreeding:

Hostage rearing projects, while intending to keep up with hereditary variety, face difficulties connected with inbreeding. Restricted genetic stocks inside hostage populaces can bring about injurious hereditary impacts, diminishing the general wellbeing and reasonability of hostage lion populaces. Cautious administration and hereditary checking are fundamental to moderate these dangers.

Business Abuse:

The business parts of keeping lions in fenced in areas, including the travel industry, prize hunting, and the outlandish pet exchange, have been dependent upon analysis. Offices that focus on financial interests over protection goals might participate in unscrupulous practices like canned hunting, where lions are reproduced for the sole reason for being pursued in restricted spaces, frequently with minimal possibility of break. Such practices compromise the honesty of real protection endeavors.

Absence of Protection Effect:

Pundits contend that the protection effect of keeping lions in fenced in areas is frequently exaggerated. While certain offices might add to reproducing projects and examination, the general commitment to the protection of wild populaces is discussed. The adequacy of renewed introduction programs, where hostage conceived lions are delivered into the wild, stays questionable and relies upon different elements, including the availability of delivered people to adjust to their common habitats.

Public Misconception:

The presence of lions in nooks can in some cases add to public false impressions about these creatures and their protection status. Guests to zoos and different offices might leave with a slanted impression of lions' normal ways of behaving, natural surroundings, and the difficulties they face in nature. Schooling programs should be vigorous to check expected misinterpretations and encourage a certifiable comprehension of the species and their protection needs.

Lacking Guideline and Oversight:

In certain districts, the absence of complete guidelines and oversight in overseeing hostage lion populaces has prompted untrustworthy practices. This incorporates deficient government assistance guidelines, reckless rearing, and sketchy associations between hostage lions and guests. Reinforcing guidelines and implementing moral principles is urgent for resolving these issues.

Influence on Wild Populaces:

Pundits contend that the accentuation on hostage reproducing and business exercises might redirect consideration and assets from tending to the underlying drivers of lion populace decrease in nature. Living space misfortune, human-natural life struggle, and poaching are huge dangers that require centered protection endeavors past hostage conditions.

Tending to the Difficulties:

Endeavors to address the difficulties and reactions related with keeping lions in nooks require a far reaching and cooperative methodology:

Further developed Fenced in area Plan:

Improvements in nook configuration are significant to furnishing hostage lions with conditions that better copy their normal environments. Bigger, more advanced spaces, open doors for mental and actual excitement, and highlights that work with regular ways of behaving are fundamental parts of further developed nooks.

Moral Rearing Practices:

Hostage reproducing programs should stick to severe moral principles to guarantee the wellbeing and hereditary variety of hostage lion populaces. Dependable rearing practices ought to focus on the protection worth of every person, staying away from rehearses that add to inbreeding or compromise the drawn out practicality of the species.

Schooling and Public Mindfulness:

Nook offices assume an imperative part in teaching people in general about lions and their protection needs. Straightforward correspondence about the difficulties looked by lions in the wild, the motivation behind hostage reproducing programs, and the significance of preservation past nooks is vital for encouraging public mindfulness and backing.

Protection Prioritization:

Protection endeavors ought to focus on tending to the main drivers of lion populace decrease in nature. This incorporates living space security, local area commitment to alleviate human-untamed life struggle, and designated enemy of poaching measures. Assets put resources into hostage conditions ought to line up with more extensive preservation objectives.

Administrative Changes:

States and preservation associations should cooperate to lay out and implement powerful guidelines overseeing the administration of hostage lion populaces. These guidelines ought to cover government assistance norms, rearing practices, and business exercises to forestall dishonest practices and guarantee the prosperity of hostage lions.

Cooperation between Partners:

Cooperation between zoological establishments, preservation associations, legislatures, and neighborhood networks is fundamental. Shared objectives and open correspondence can prompt more compelling protection procedures that think about the more extensive setting of lion preservation, both in bondage and in nature.

Chapter 2

Understanding Lion Behavior

Lions (Panthera leo) are notorious enormous felines and an image of force, strength, and magnificence. As dominant hunters, lions assume a urgent part in keeping up with the natural equilibrium of their territories. Understanding lion conduct is fundamental for preservation endeavors, guaranteeing the prosperity of hostage populaces, and upgrading conjunction among lions and human networks. This exhaustive investigation digs into different parts of lion conduct, including social design, correspondence, hunting methodologies, and the elements impacting their conduct in both wild and hostage settings.

1. **Social Construction and Collective vibes:**
   Lions are known for their social nature, living in bunches called prides. The social construction of lions is mind boggling and assumes a fundamental part in their endurance and propagation. Key parts of lion social way of behaving include:
   Pride Design:
   A pride commonly comprises of related females and their posterity, with a prevailing male known as the pride's chief. Subordinate

guys may likewise be available, framing collusions with the prevailing male. Prides show a steady and helpful social design, with females frequently staying in the natal pride and guys scattering as they arrive at development.

Job of Predominant Guys:

Predominant guys assume a critical part in shielding the pride's region, which incorporates prime hunting grounds and assets. They likewise add to shielding fledglings from possible dangers, including rival guys looking to assume control over the pride.

Helpful Hunting:

Lions are known for their helpful hunting conduct. The cooperation inside prides improves the probability of fruitful kills, particularly while focusing on bigger prey. Helpful hunting permits lions to bring down prey that would be moving for a solitary lion to catch.

Social Bonds:

Solid social bonds exist inside prides, especially among related females. These bonds add to agreeable nurturing, where lionesses on the whole consideration for and safeguard the pride's offspring. Social attachment upgrades the general achievement and strength of the pride.

2. **Correspondence and Vocalizations:**

Lions utilize different vocalizations and non-vocal specialized techniques to pass on data, keep up with social bonds, and direction bunch exercises. Understanding these correspondence signals is essential for unraveling the complicated elements inside prides:

Thundering:

Thundering is an unmistakable vocalization related with lions, frequently utilized by guys to declare strength and convey their presence to equal guys. Thunders are likewise utilized for the purpose of publicizing an area and drawing in possible mates.

Vocalizations of Whelps:

Lion whelps speak with their moms and kin through a scope of vocalizations, including mewing, murmuring, and snarling. These vocalizations act as fundamental types of correspondence, assisting whelps with remaining associated with the pride and request consideration from grown-ups.

Contact Calls:

Lions use contact calls to find each other inside the thick vegetation of their territories. These calls assist with keeping up with bunch union, particularly during exercises like hunting or when isolated individuals need to rejoin.

Groaning and Murmuring:

Lions radiate groans and murmurs, especially during social communications and holding minutes. These sounds add to supporting social bonds and can be seen between grown-up lions and among grown-ups and fledglings.

Looks and Non-verbal communication:

Non-vocal correspondence, including looks and non-verbal communication, is vital to lion connections. Looks, for example, head scouring and licking convey connection, while tail developments and stances impart a scope of feelings, from unwinding to sharpness.

3. **Regenerative Way of behaving:**

Regenerative conduct in lions is firmly connected to their social construction, and understanding the complexities of lion proliferation is fundamental for guaranteeing the supportability of wild populaces:

Estrus Cycles in Females:

Female lions experience estrus cycles, regularly happening each a little while. During estrus, females show open ways of behaving, taking into account mating with the prevailing male. The synchronization of estrus cycles inside a pride frequently prompts various females conceiving an offspring around a similar time.

Mating Conduct:

Mating includes romance customs, vocalizations, and relations. The prevailing male mates with responsive females, building up friendly bonds and attesting his conceptive predominance inside the pride.

Incubation and Birth:

The incubation time frame for lions is about 110 days. Lionesses bring forth litters of one to four whelps, and the whole pride is engaged with really focusing on and safeguarding the weak fledglings. Agreeable nurturing upgrades the whelps' possibilities of endurance.

Child murder:

In specific circumstances, approaching guys might participate in child murder, killing the posterity of the past prevailing male. This conduct is remembered to speed up the females' re-visitation of estrus, empowering the novice to sire his own posterity.

4. **Hunting Techniques and Taking care of Conduct:**

Lions are gifted trackers, utilizing different systems and procedures to get prey. Their hunting conduct is molded by variables like gathering coordination, prey accessibility, and the size and period of individual lions:

Agreeable Hunting:

Helpful hunting is a sign of lion conduct. The cooperative endeavors of the pride increment the possibilities of an effective chase, especially while focusing on bigger herbivores. Lions utilize facilitated strategies to encompass and snare their prey.

Following and Ambushing:

Lions are proficient stalkers, utilizing vegetation and the territory to cover their methodology. The component of shock is critical, and lions frequently depend on covertness and tolerance prior to sending off a trap. The nearness of pride individuals takes into account compelling coordination during an assault.

Prey Determination:

Lions are sharp hunters with a shifted diet that incorporates wildebeest, zebras, impalas, and different ungulates. The decision of prey is impacted by variables, for example, accessibility, crowd size, and the presence of weak people, like adolescents or debilitated grown-ups.

Rummaging Conduct:

Lions are additionally known to search, deftly benefiting from cadavers deserted by different hunters or regular causes. Rummaging permits lions to save energy and exploit accessible assets.

Taking care of Order:

The social design of prides stretches out to taking care of order. Prevailing people, especially the pride guys, frequently have need admittance to the corpse. Subordinate individuals, including lionesses and whelps, may hang tight or feed on leftovers after the prevailing people have eaten.

5. **Regional Way of behaving and Home Reach:**

Lions show regional way of behaving for the purpose of getting assets and keeping up with command over their environmental factors. Territoriality is affected by elements, for example, prey accessibility, water sources, and the presence of contending prides:

Regional Stamping:

Lions mark their domains through different means, including aroma checking and pee splashing. This conduct conveys the presence of the pride, dissuades gatecrashers, and assumes a part in keeping up with social union inside the pride.

Regional Size:

The size of a lion pride's domain is variable and impacted by elements like prey thickness and living space quality. Bigger domains are by and large connected with more bountiful prey assets. Regional limits are effectively safeguarded against rival prides.

Intraspecific Animosity:

Connections between adjoining prides can prompt forceful experiences, especially when domains cross-over. These showdowns might include vocalizations, actual showdowns, and, surprisingly, deadly battles between predominant guys from rival prides.

Migrant Way of behaving:

In specific circumstances, especially when prides become excessively huge or assets become scant, lions might display migrant way of behaving. Itinerant people might wander outside customary regions looking for food and appropriate natural surroundings.

6. **Transformations to Living space and Natural Variables:**

Lion conduct is formed by the assorted scope of living spaces they occupy, from savannas and fields to forests and semi-deserts. Understanding how lions adjust to their surroundings is essential for compelling protection and the executives:

Nighttime Conduct:

Lions are crepuscular and nighttime trackers, displaying increased action during the cooler long stretches of first light and nightfall. This conduct assists them with keeping away from the intensity of the day and exploit decreased perceivability for hunting.

Water Reliance:

While lions can get by for expanded periods without water, they are known to be water-subordinate contrasted with other huge felines. Admittance to water sources impacts their selection of regions and adds to their outcome in assorted living spaces.

Climatic Transformations:

Lions are adjusted to a scope of environments, from the hot and parched districts to additional mild conditions. Their fur hue and thickness differ, with lions in dry areas frequently having lighter coats to effectively disseminate heat more.

Cover and Trap Strategies:

The coat example of lions, described by a blend of brownish tones and troublesome markings, gives successful disguise in their normal territories. This cover supports following and ambushing prey.

7. **Lion Conduct in Bondage:**

Understanding lion conduct in hostage settings is urgent for guaranteeing the government assistance of these creatures and the progress of hostage reproducing and preservation programs. Hostage conditions present special difficulties and contemplations:

Walled in area Plan:

Walled in areas in imprisonment should repeat the common habitat of lions as intently as could be expected. Sufficient room, ecological improvement, and amazing open doors for mental and actual feeling are fundamental for the prosperity of hostage lions.

Social Elements in Imprisonment:

Overseeing social elements in hostage settings requires cautious thought. Dwelling together of viable people, thoughtfulness regarding the social construction inside a gathering, and limiting stressors add to positive social connections.

Taking care of and Enhancement:

Hostage lions should get a reasonable and healthfully suitable eating regimen. Improvement exercises, like riddle feeders, novel items, and tangible feeling, are vital for forestalling weariness and advancing normal ways of behaving.

Conceptive Administration:

Hostage rearing projects require cautious conceptive administration to keep away from inbreeding and keep up with hereditary variety. Managed impregnation and controlled rearing projects might be executed to accomplish protection objectives.

Social Observing:

Social observing is fundamental in imprisonment to survey the prosperity of lions. Noticing ways of behaving connected with pressure, wellbeing, and social communications assists guardians with giving ideal consideration and mediate when vital.

2.1 Natural habitat and behavior of wild lions

Lions (Panthera leo), frequently alluded to as the "lord of the wilderness," are glorious animals that have spellbound human interest for a really long time. Their regular environment and conduct are complicatedly connected to the biological systems they occupy, and understanding these perspectives is essential for compelling protection and the executives. In this investigation, we dig into the normal territory and conduct of wild lions, revealing insight into the many-sided elements that characterize their reality in nature.

1. **Normal Living space:**

   Wild lions are local to different living spaces across Africa, going from savannas and meadows to forests and semi-deserts. Their versatility to different conditions adds to their inescapable dispersion on the landmass. Key elements of their normal territory include:

   Savannas and Prairies:

   Lions are frequently connected with the immense savannas of Africa. These open scenes give ideal circumstances to hunting, permitting lions to utilize their sharp vision to detect prey from a good ways. The overflow of herbivores in savannas supports lion populaces and supports their agreeable hunting conduct.

   Forests and Clean:

   Lions likewise occupy lush regions and scrublands, where vegetation might be denser than in open savannas. These conditions offer open doors for subtle following and ambushing prey, using the cover given by trees and hedges.

   Desert and Semi-Desert Areas:

   In certain areas, lions have adjusted to dry conditions, including deserts and semi-deserts. These transformations might incorporate lighter coats to disseminate heat effectively and a capacity to get by for stretched out periods without admittance to water.

   Water Sources:

   While lions can get through periods without water, they are water-subordinate contrasted with other huge felines. Admittance to water sources, like streams and watering openings, impacts the choice of domains and adds to the general progress of lion populaces in their natural surroundings.

Regional Reach:

The regional scope of a lion pride shifts in light of elements like prey accessibility, water sources, and rivalry with adjoining prides. Domains are effectively shielded against interlopers, and the size can go from a couple of square miles to bigger territories, contingent upon ecological elements.

2. **Social Design and Conduct:**

The social design and conduct of wild lions are portrayed by mind boggling elements that have advanced for endurance and conceptive achievement. Key parts of their way of behaving include:

Pride Design:

Lions display a social design based on prides, which ordinarily comprise of related females and their posterity. A prevailing male, frequently connected with the expression "pride pioneer," directs the gathering. Subordinate guys might shape collusions with the prevailing male or move between prides.

Helpful Hunting:

One of the most notable ways of behaving of lions is their agreeable hunting. Cooperating as a pride improves the probability of effective kills, especially while focusing on bigger prey. Agreeable hunting includes composed systems, with lions taking on unambiguous jobs during an assault.

Regional Checking:

Lions mark their regions through different means, including fragrance checking and pee showering. Regional stamping fills the double need of conveying the presence of the pride and stopping rival prides or people from infringing an on their area.

Nighttime Conduct:

Lions are crepuscular and nighttime trackers, displaying increased movement during the cooler long periods of day break and night-fall. Nighttime conduct assists lions with keeping away from the intensity of the day and exploit decreased perceivability for hunting.

Social Bonds and Association:

Solid social bonds exist inside prides, especially among related females. Social attachment adds to agreeable nurturing, where lionesses all in all consideration for and safeguard the pride's whelps. Affiliative ways of behaving, for example, preparing and head scouring, support social bonds.

Regenerative Way of behaving:

Regenerative conduct in lions is firmly connected to their social design. Female lions experience estrus cycles, during which they display open ways of behaving. Mating includes romance ceremonies, vocalizations, and lovemaking. The synchronization of estrus cycles inside a pride frequently prompts different females conceiving an offspring around a similar time.

Nurturing and Helpful Fledgling Consideration:

Nurturing liabilities are shared inside the pride, with helpful consideration for offspring being an outstanding way of behaving. Lionesses all in all safeguard and support the pride's posterity, adding to the fledglings' possibilities of endurance.

3. **Hunting Procedures and Taking care of Conduct:**

Lions are dominant hunters with a different eating routine that incorporates a scope of herbivores. Their hunting procedures and taking care of conduct are finely tuned to augment progress in nature:

Composed Assaults:

Helpful hunting includes facilitated assaults on prey. Lions use cooperation to encompass and snare bigger herbivores, using their solidarity and numbers to beat the prey's guards.

Following and Ambushing:

Lions are gifted stalkers, utilizing vegetation and the territory to disguise their methodology. The component of shock is critical, and lions frequently depend on secrecy and persistence prior to sending off a snare. The closeness of pride individuals considers compelling coordination during an assault.

Prey Determination:

Lions are deft hunters with a differed diet that incorporates wildebeest, zebras, impalas, and different ungulates. The decision of prey is affected by elements, for example, accessibility, crowd size, and the presence of weak people, like adolescents or debilitated grown-ups.

Rummaging Conduct:

Lions are additionally known to rummage, deftly benefiting from corpses deserted by different hunters or normal causes. Rummaging permits lions to preserve energy and exploit accessible assets.

Taking care of Order:

Social elements reach out to taking care of pecking order inside the pride. Predominant people, especially the pride guys, frequently have need admittance to the body. Subordinate individuals, including lionesses and fledglings, may hang tight or feed on leftovers after the predominant people have eaten.

4. **Dangers to Wild Lions and Preservation Difficulties:**

While wild lions have adjusted to their indigenous habitats over centuries, they face various dangers that challenge their endurance. Preservation challenges include:

Living space Misfortune and Discontinuity:

Human exercises, including horticulture and urbanization, lead to natural surroundings misfortune and discontinuity. Diminished accessible space can influence lion populaces, restricting their admittance to prey and water sources.

Human-Untamed life Struggle:

As human populaces grow, clashes among people and lions raise. Animals theft by lions frequently brings about retaliatory killings by nearby networks, representing a danger to lion populaces.

Poaching and Unlawful Untamed life Exchange:

Poaching for lion parts, like bones and skins, as well as the unlawful exchange live whelps, represents a critical danger to wild lion populaces. Interest for these things is driven by social convictions, prize hunting, and the colorful pet exchange.

Sickness Flare-ups:

Lions are defenseless to sicknesses that can wreck populaces. The spread of infections, frequently worked with by human exercises and the nearness of homegrown creatures to natural life, represents a danger to the wellbeing and endurance of lion populaces.

Environmental Change:

Environmental change can modify biological systems and upset prey-hunter connections. Lions might confront moves in adjusting to changing ecological circumstances, influencing their endurance.

2.2 The impact of captivity on lion behavior

Lions, adored as images of solidarity and grandness, dazzle the creative mind and interest of individuals all over the planet. While wild lions possess assorted biological systems and show complex ways of behaving formed by their common habitat, the elements of lion conduct go through huge changes when these creatures are exposed to bondage. This investigation dives into the effect of imprisonment on lion conduct, unwinding the difficulties, transformations, and protection suggestions related with lodging these brilliant hunters in restricted conditions.

1. **The Difficulties of Bondage:**
   Restricted Space and Conduct Articulation:
   One of the main difficulties of bondage for lions is the limitation of room. In the wild, lions meander huge regions, participate in complex social designs, and display a scope of regular ways of behaving fundamental for their prosperity.
   Repression to walled in areas confines the outflow of these ways of behaving, prompting expected disappointment, stress, and the advancement of stereotypic ways of behaving.

Social Elements and Gathering Design:

Lions in the wild live in prides, showing mind boggling social elements and helpful ways of behaving. In imprisonment, the development of fake prides or the gathering of irrelevant people might upset these regular social designs. Bound spaces can bring about expanded contest for assets, hostility, and difficulties in laying out a firm collective vibe.

Counterfeit Conditions and Boosts:

Hostage conditions frequently miss the mark on intricacy and variety of the normal living spaces that lions have advanced to explore. The shortfall of fluctuated scenes, vegetation, and the potential chance to draw in with a changing climate can prompt tangible hardship and an absence of mental excitement. Lions might become exhausted and fretful, provoking the appearance of strange ways of behaving.

Taking care of Difficulties and Stereotypic Ways of behaving:

In imprisonment, lions are given a controlled eating routine, frequently comprising of financially pre-arranged food. This differentiations with the unusualness and difficulties related with chasing after food in nature. The absence of chances for hunting and the utilization of entire prey can add to weariness and the advancement of stereotypic ways of behaving, like pacing or monotonous developments.

Absence of Physical and Mental Difficulties:

Lions are clever and genuinely proficient hunters that flourish with difficulties. In bondage, where endurance necessities are ensured, the shortfall of physical and mental difficulties can prompt the underutilization of their regular impulses. Taking part in ways of behaving like hunting, investigating, and critical thinking becomes restricted, influencing both physical and mental prosperity.

2. **Conduct Transformations in Imprisonment:**

Adjusted Conceptive Ways of behaving:

Hostage conditions might impact the conceptive ways of behaving of lions. Changes in friendly elements, walled in area plan, and the accessibility of mates can affect estrus cycles, mating ways of behaving, and regenerative achievement. Now and again, hostage lions might show different conceptive examples contrasted with their wild partners.

Changes in Hunting Ways of behaving:

The absence of hunting valuable open doors in bondage requires changes in hunting ways of behaving. A few hostage lions might take part in mock hunting ways of behaving or play exercises that imitate components of hunting. Giving advancement exercises, like riddle feeders, can empower critical thinking and animate hunting-related ways of behaving.

Connections with People:

Lions in bondage frequently have normal connections with people, including guardians, veterinarians, and guests. While positive connections can add to socialization and conduct improvement, negative cooperations or openness to inordinate human presence might prompt pressure and adjusted ways of behaving.

Expanded Resistance to Nearness:

Hostage lions might display expanded resistance to human presence, as they become acquainted with customary contact from overseers and guests. While this transformation can upgrade open doors for instructive and research drives, it likewise presents gambles, as lions might lose their regular watchfulness of people.

Changes in Rest Examples:

Lions in the wild are known for their crepuscular and night-time hunting ways of behaving. In bondage, where taking care of timetables and guest collaborations might happen over the course of the day, lions might change their rest designs. A few hostage lions might turn out to be more diurnal, modifying their normal action cycle.

3. **Preservation Suggestions:**

Hereditary Variety and Hostage Reproducing Projects:

Hostage conditions assume a significant part in preservation endeavors, especially in keeping up with hereditary variety and forestalling the deficiency of one of a kind genealogies. Mindful hostage reproducing programs intend to guarantee the wellbeing and reasonability of hostage lion populaces. Notwithstanding, difficulties, for example, inbreeding risk and the restricted genetic stock inside hostage populaces need cautious administration.

Training and Public Mindfulness:

Hostage lions add to instruction and public mindfulness about the difficulties confronting wild lion populaces. Zoos and asylums give valuable chances to individuals to find out about the significance of protection, the dangers confronting lions, and the job people can play in preservation endeavors. Very much oversaw hostage conditions can motivate a feeling of sympathy and obligation toward wild partners.

Research Open doors:

Hostage conditions give controlled settings to logical examination on lion conduct, propagation, and wellbeing. Concentrating on hostage lions can yield important bits of knowledge that might illuminate preservation methodologies for wild populaces. Research in imprisonment can likewise add to progressions in veterinary consideration and the comprehension of lion physiology.

Emergency Reaction and Restoration:

Hostage offices, especially safe-havens, frequently assume a vital part in giving crisis care and recovery to lions saved from critical circumstances, like unlawful dealing or harmful imprisonment. These offices offer another opportunity for lions to carry on with a more normal life subsequent to encountering injury or abuse.

Renewed introduction Projects:

A few hostage conceived lions are possibility for renewed introduction into nature. Renewed introduction programs plan to reinforce wild populaces by delivering hostage conceived people into appropriate living spaces. While these projects can possibly add to the rebuilding of environmental equilibrium, they require fastidious preparation and thought of different variables, remembering the availability of lions for life for nature.

4. **Moral Contemplations and Best Practices:**

Accommodating Treatment and Government assistance Principles:

Moral contemplations in hostage lion the executives spin around inquiries of creature government assistance, regular way of behaving, and the effect of constrainment on physical and mental wellbeing. Hostage offices should focus on the prosperity of lions, guaranteeing that nooks meet or surpass laid out government assistance guidelines.

Straightforwardness and Responsibility:

Zoos, asylums, and rearing offices should work straightforwardly and be responsible for their activities. Open correspondence about protection objectives, reproducing rehearses, and the treatment of individual lions cultivates trust among the general population and preservation partners.

Mindful Rearing Practices:

Hostage reproducing projects ought to stick to dependable practices to keep away from inbreeding and keep up with hereditary variety. Reproducing ought to line up with preservation objectives, and surplus creatures shouldn't add to issues, for example, overpopulation or unscrupulous practices like canned hunting.

Training and Preservation Informing:

Hostage offices ought to focus on instruction and protection informing. Guests ought to leave with a more noteworthy comprehension of the difficulties confronting lions in the wild and a feeling of obligation for their preservation. Instruction projects can dissipate legends, bring issues to light about dangers, and move activity.

Social Improvement and Walled in area Plan:

To address the difficulties of imprisonment, offices should focus on conduct improvement and insightful fenced in area plan. Giving open doors to mental and actual feeling, recreating regular highlights, and empowering normal ways of behaving add to the prosperity of hostage lions.

2.3 Psychological and physical effects of enclosure life

The nook life of hostage lions, whether in zoos, safe-havens, or reproducing offices, achieves a mind boggling exchange of mental and actual consequences for these glorious hunters. While bondage fills different needs, including protection, schooling, and exploration, it is fundamental to basically inspect the effect of repression on the prosperity of lions. This investigation dives into the mental and actual impacts of fenced in area life, revealing insight into the difficulties and contemplations related with lodging lions in restricted spaces.

1. **Mental Impacts:**
   Restricted Social Articulation:
   One of the essential mental difficulties for hostage lions is the limitation of regular ways of behaving because of restricted space. In the wild, lions wander tremendous domains, participate in friendly collaborations, and display a great many ways of behaving fundamental for their psychological prosperity. Constrainment to fenced in areas frequently reduces these regular ways of behaving, prompting pressure and dissatisfaction.

   Improvement of Stereotypic Ways of behaving:
   Stereotypic ways of behaving, like pacing, monotonous developments, or self-preparing extravagantly, are normal in hostage lions. These ways of behaving are demonstrative of mental pain and can emerge because of fatigue, dissatisfaction, or an absence of feeling. Stereotypic ways of behaving are viewed as maladaptive reactions to the difficulties of bondage.

   Social Disturbance:
   Lions are social creatures that flourish with complex social

designs. In imprisonment, the gathering of irrelevant people or the development of fake prides might disturb normal social elements. This can prompt expanded rivalry for assets, animosity, and difficulties in laying out and keeping up with durable social bonds.

Adapting to Restricted Improvement:

Improvement exercises are vital for the mental prosperity of hostage lions. Nonetheless, giving compelling improvement in fenced in areas can challenge. The shortfall of normal improvements, like shifted scenes and hunting open doors, expects guardians to devise imaginative and invigorating advancement techniques to connect with lions intellectually and truly.

Stress and Tension:

Repression, the presence of human guests, and changes in day to day schedules can prompt pressure and uneasiness in hostage lions. Raised feelings of anxiety might appear in physiological changes, modified rest designs, and conduct reactions characteristic of mental uneasiness.

2. **Actual Impacts:**

Decreased Actual Wellness:

Imprisonment to fenced in areas restricts the chance for normal proactive tasks like hunting, following, and regional watching. Therefore, hostage lions might encounter diminished actual wellness, prompting muscle decay and diminished in general wellbeing. The absence of room for meandering and investigation further adds to a stationary way of life.

Heftiness and Overweight:

In bondage, lions might confront difficulties connected with weight the executives. Restricted space for development and a controlled eating regimen given via overseers can add to weight and overweight circumstances. Stoutness presents wellbeing chances, influencing organ capability, joint wellbeing, and in general imperativeness.

Dental and Oral Medical problems:

Hostage lions might display dental and oral medical conditions because of variables, for example, an absence of regular chewing on bones and dental difficulties related with counterfeit weight control plans. These issues can bring about tooth rot, gum infection, and inconvenience, influencing the general wellbeing and life span of hostage lions.

Regenerative Difficulties:

The changed social elements and natural states of imprisonment can impact the regenerative strength of lions. Issues, for example, upset estrus cycles, troubles in mating ways of behaving, and challenges in raising fledglings in hostage settings can affect the regenerative progress of hostage lion populaces.

Disabled Resistant Capability:

Stress, restricted development, and possible openness to infections inside hostage conditions can think twice about resistant capability of lions. Debilitated safe frameworks make hostage lions more defenseless to contaminations and infections, influencing their general wellbeing and strength.

3. **Protection and Moral Contemplations:**

Adjusting Protection Objectives and Government assistance:

Hostage conditions assume a part in protection endeavors, especially in keeping up with hereditary variety and giving a security net to imperiled species. Nonetheless, a sensitive equilibrium should be struck between preservation objectives and the government assistance of individual creatures. Mindful hostage the executives focuses on the wellbeing and prosperity of lions while adding to more extensive protection targets.

Straightforwardness and Moral Practices:

The moral treatment of hostage lions requests straightforwardness and adherence to elevated requirements of care. Zoos, safe-havens, and rearing offices should work morally, guaranteeing that fenced in areas meet or surpass laid out government assistance guidelines. Open correspondence about the treatment of creatures and preservation informing encourages trust among general society and protection partners.

Instructive Drives:

Hostage lions give valuable open doors to instructive drives that bring issues to light about the difficulties confronting wild lion populaces. Zoos and safe-havens can assume a pivotal part in motivating sympathy, scattering legends, and teaching general society about the significance of preservation endeavors.

Consistent Improvement and Exploration:

The comprehension of the mental and actual impacts of fenced in area life on lions advances with progressing research and persistent improvement in hostage the executives rehearses. Research in bondage can add to headways in veterinary consideration, conduct science, and preservation methodologies for both hostage and wild populaces.

2.4 Scientific studies on captive lion behavior

Logical examinations on hostage lion conduct have given important experiences into the perplexing elements of these glorious hunters inside constrainment. Scientists have dove into different perspectives, including the mental prosperity, social collaborations, and versatile ways of behaving displayed by lions in bondage.

Concentrates frequently center around the effect of nook plan on lion conduct, analyzing how different spatial courses of action, ecological enhancement, and social groupings impact their general government assistance. Perceptions of stereotypic ways of behaving, like pacing or dull developments, add to understanding the stressors related with hostage life.

Besides, specialists investigate what hostage conditions mean for conceptive ways of behaving, mating designs, and nurturing elements among lions. Researching the adequacy of advancement exercises, for example, novel improvements or taking care of difficulties, creates techniques to upgrade the psychological excitement and generally fulfillment of hostage lions.

Logical investigation into hostage lion conduct not just guides in refining hostage the executives rehearses for the government assistance of individual lions yet in addition adds to more extensive protection objectives and our comprehension of these dominant hunters' transformations to fake conditions. The discoveries guide moral practices in zoos, asylums, and reproducing programs, guaranteeing that imprisonment lines up with the wellbeing of the lions under human consideration.

3

Chapter 3

The Call for Change

The call for change reverberations through the halls of history, flagging mankind's consistent development and the tenacious quest for a superior, more evenhanded world. This thorough investigation digs into the diverse elements of the call for change, looking at its authentic roots, the socio-social elements that impel it, the job of backing and activism, and the extraordinary effect on people and social orders.

1. **Authentic Points of view on Change:**
   Ages of Upheaval:
   Change has been an enduring power in mankind's set of experiences, frequently solidified in snapshots of transformation. From the Renaissance to the Modern Upset, seismic changes in thought, innovation, and social designs have reshaped the direction of civilizations.
   Social Developments:
   The call for change finds articulation in different social developments that challenge existing standards and supporter for equity, uniformity, and basic liberties. Models incorporate the

social equality development, women's activist developments, and LGBTQ+ freedoms activism, each making a permanent imprint on the shared perspective.

Political Changes:

The battle for political change has been a main thrust behind the ascent and fall of countries. Autonomy developments, hostile to provincial battles, and the push for a majority rules system highlight the getting through journey for self-assurance and administration established in the desire of individuals.

2. **Cultural Elements and Impetuses for Change:**

Social Movements:

Changes in social standards, values, and mentalities frequently act as impetuses for more extensive cultural changes. Advancing viewpoints on issues like orientation jobs, variety, and ecological awareness mirror the effect of social movements on the call for change.

Innovative Headways:

The fast speed of innovative advancement reshapes the manner in which social orders capability and convey. The coming of the web, virtual entertainment, and advanced stages has intensified voices, worked with worldwide network, and excited developments for change.

Globalization and Interconnectedness:

Globalization has obscured public limits, encouraging interconnectedness and reliance. Difficulties, for example, environmental change, pandemics, and financial differences request aggregate reactions, driving a worldwide call for change.

Segment Advances:

Evolving socioeconomics, remembering shifts for populace age, urbanization, and relocation designs, add to the recalibration of cultural standards and needs. Youth-drove developments frequently arise as strong influencers, testing settled in frameworks and pushing for a more comprehensive future.

3. **Support and Activism:**

Force of Grassroots Developments:

Grassroots developments assume a vital part in enhancing the call for change. From neighborhood local area drives to worldwide missions, grassroots activism enables people to resolve issues going from natural preservation to civil rights.

Job of Support Associations:

Support associations act as impetuses for change by utilizing assets, leading exploration, and participating in designated crusades. NGOs, non-benefits, and backing bunches champion causes going from basic liberties to medical services change, driving fundamental change.

Media and Data Scattering:

The media's part in forming stories and dispersing data is urgent in catalyzing cultural change. Analytical news-casting, narratives, and virtual entertainment activism add to public mindfulness and activation.

Legitimate Promotion:

Legitimate promotion fills in as a foundation for institutional change. Court fights and lawful difficulties have been instrumental in accomplishing milestone choices that advance social equality, ecological assurances, and other key cultural changes.

4. **Extraordinary Effect on People:**

Strengthening and Organization:

The call for change enables people, imparting a feeling of organization and obligation. Activism permits individuals to become engineers of their predeterminations, cultivating a feeling of support and commitment to molding their general surroundings.

Mental Movements:

Openness to different points of view and the call for change frequently hasten mental movements. People rethink their convictions, stand up to inclinations, and embrace more comprehensive perspectives, adding to a more extensive cultural change.

Flexibility and Versatility:

Exploring change requires flexibility and versatility. People who notice the call for change foster survival techniques, versatility despite affliction, and the capacity to adjust to advancing conditions.

Municipal Commitment and Social Obligation:

The call for change empowers municipal commitment and a feeling of social obligation. People effectively take part in local area drives, volunteerism, and political cycles to add to positive cultural changes.

5. **Provokes and Protection from Change:**

Institutional Latency:

Establishments, whether legislative, corporate, or social, frequently oppose change because of settled in interests, regulatory dormancy, or anxiety toward disturbance. Beating institutional opposition requires supported endeavors and key promotion.

Social Kickback:

The call for change can set off social reaction from people and gatherings who see their qualities or honors as under danger. Exploring social opposition includes encouraging discourse, compassion, and schooling to connect partitions.

Financial Inconsistencies:

Financial inconsistencies can be both a reason and an outcome of the call for change. Variations in riches and assets might fuel social agitation, while endeavors for change might confront obstruction from those trying to safeguard existing financial progressive systems.

Political Resistance:

Political powers impervious to change might capitalize on their leverage to frustrate moderate developments. This resistance highlights the inborn difficulties in exploring the crossing point of governmental issues and the call for cultural change.

6. **The Multifacetedness of Progress:**
Multifaceted Backing:

The call for change is innately diverse, perceiving the interconnected idea of social issues. Developments that embrace interconnection address the covering aspects of character, honor, and persecution, cultivating more comprehensive and viable promotion.

Ecological Equity:

The ecological call for change features the earnestness of tending to environmental change, biodiversity misfortune, and feasible asset the executives. Natural equity developments underscore the lopsided effect of biological issues on underestimated networks.

Social and Racial Value:

The call for social and racial value highlights the need to destroy fundamental prejudice and make comprehensive social orders. Developments like People of color Matter supporter for equity, balance, and the acknowledgment of the intrinsic worth of each and every person.

Orientation Uniformity and LGBTQ+ Freedoms:

The call for orientation uniformity and LGBTQ+ freedoms challenges instilled standards and backers for an additional comprehensive and evenhanded world. Developments supporting these makes look for destroy oppressive practices and cultivate acknowledgment and equivalent open doors.

7. **The Worldwide Call for Change:**
Transnational Developments:

The call for change rises above public boundaries, leading to transnational developments that join individuals in a common quest for equity, basic freedoms, and ecological maintainability. Issues like evacuee privileges, worldwide wellbeing, and harmony building request cooperative, worldwide reactions.

Global Participation:

Worldwide associations, political endeavors, and cooperative arrangements assume a pivotal part in answering the worldwide call for change.

Tending to difficulties, for example, environmental change, pandemics, and philanthropic emergencies requires composed activity on a worldwide scale.

Computerized Activism and Worldwide Availability:

Computerized activism outfits the force of innovation to intensify the worldwide call for change. Online entertainment stages give a space to people overall to interface, share data, and prepare support for different causes.

Compassionate Reactions:

Philanthropic endeavors answer emergencies and crises, epitomizing the worldwide call for empathy and fortitude. Associations and people participated in philanthropic place of business issues going from struggle prompted uprooting to catastrophic events.

8. **The Development of Progress:**

Adjusting to Contemporary Difficulties:

The call for change keeps on developing as contemporary difficulties arise. Issues like computerized reasoning morals, bioethics, and the moral ramifications of mechanical progressions require continuous variation in support and cultural reactions.

The Job of Training:

Training fills in as an impetus for change by cultivating decisive reasoning, compassion, and a feeling of social obligation. Educational plans that address different points of view, authentic treacheries, and worldwide difficulties add to making educated and enabled people.

Youth-Drove Developments:

Youth-drove developments, driven by enthusiasm and a need to keep moving, have arisen as powerful influencers. From environment strikes to civil rights backing, youthful activists assume an essential part in molding the story and driving cultural change.

The Call for Fundamental Change:

Past resolving individual issues, the call for change progressively stresses the requirement for foundational changes. Developments advocate for rebuilding financial frameworks, reconsidering administration, and destroying institutional hindrances to make all the more and supportable social orders.

3.1 Growing awareness of the need for better lion welfare

Lately, there has been a huge flood in mindfulness in regards to the government assistance of lions, mirroring a worldwide acknowledgment of the difficulties these grand animals face in imprisonment and nature.

The call for better lion government assistance originates from a profound comprehension of the intricate requirements and ways of behaving of these dominant hunters. This investigation digs into the variables adding to the developing attention to the requirement for better lion government assistance, looking at the difficulties lions experience in bondage and their normal environments. It additionally addresses the developing job of preservation, moral contemplations, and the aggregate liability to guarantee the prosperity of lions notwithstanding expanding dangers.

1. **Bondage and the Call for Moral Treatment:**
   Zoos and Hostage Offices:
   The job of zoos and hostage offices in lion government assistance has been a subject of expanding examination. As mindfulness develops, so does the interest for moral treatment inside these organizations. Concerns range from nook size and natural enhancement to rearing practices and the generally mental and actual prosperity of lions.
   Stereotypic Ways of behaving and Stress:
   Lions in imprisonment frequently show stereotypic ways of behaving, for example, pacing or dreary developments, which are characteristic of stress and dissatisfaction. Developing mindfulness has prompted a basic assessment of the circumstances that add to these ways of behaving, inciting calls for further developed

nooks, improvement, and better administration rehearses.

Hostage Rearing and Preservation Morals:

The hostage rearing of lions, frequently connected with business interests, for example, prize hunting and the fascinating pet exchange, has raised moral worries. The consciousness of the likely adverse consequence on wild populaces, hereditary variety, and the prosperity of hostage people has filled a call for additional dependable reproducing rehearses and a reconsideration of the job of hostage lions in protection endeavors.

Popular Assessment and Backfire:

Public mindfulness and opinion assume a significant part in forming the talk on lion government assistance. Examples of creature abuse, disregard, or questionable practices in imprisonment have prompted public kickback and escalated the call for moral treatment. Web-based entertainment and expanded network add to the spread of data and the preparation of popular assessment.

2. **Preservation Difficulties and the Situation of Wild Lions:**

Living space Misfortune and Discontinuity:

Lions face extreme dangers in their regular natural surroundings, fundamentally because of living space misfortune and fracture brought about by human exercises. The transformation of land for agribusiness, urbanization, and foundation advancement reduces the accessible space for lions, prompting expanded human-untamed life struggle and compromising the general prosperity of wild populaces.

Human-Natural life Struggle:

As human populaces venture into lion domains, clashes emerge over assets and land. Retaliatory killings of lions because of domesticated animals ravaging or saw dangers to human security further fuel the difficulties looked by these hunters. Developing mindfulness underlines the requirement for conjunction procedures and struggle moderation measures.

Poaching and Unlawful Untamed life Exchange:

Poaching for lion parts, like bones and skins, and the unlawful untamed life exchange present critical dangers to lion populaces. The interest for these things is in many cases energized by social convictions, prize hunting, and the extraordinary pet exchange. The call for better lion government assistance incorporates endeavors to battle poaching and the unlawful exchange that risk the endurance of wild lion populaces.

Illness Flare-ups and Preservation Wellbeing:

Lions are vulnerable to sicknesses that can decimate populaces. The spread of infections, frequently worked with by human exercises and the nearness of homegrown creatures to untamed life, represents a danger to the wellbeing and preservation of lion populaces. Developing mindfulness underlines the significance of extensive wellbeing the executives in lion preservation.

3. **Moral Contemplations in Preservation:**

Prize Hunting and Game:

The morals of prize hunting, wherein lions are pursued for sport, has ignited banters on the effect of such practices on individual lions and populaces. The call for better lion government assistance incorporates a reassessment of prize hunting works on, taking into account the biological job of lions and the moral ramifications of seeking after them as prizes.

Canned Hunting Debate:

Canned hunting, where lions are reproduced in imprisonment for the sole reason for being pursued in restricted spaces, has been a wellspring of moral concern.

The mindfulness encompassing this training has prompted expanded investigation, with advocates requiring a finish to canned hunting and the execution of stricter guidelines.

Extraordinary Pet Exchange:

The extraordinary pet exchange represents a danger to lion government assistance, as whelps are frequently taken advantage of for business gain. Developing mindfulness stresses the need to battle the interest for extraordinary pets and the related issues of inappropriate consideration, unlawful dealing, and the propagation of the pattern of hostage reproducing.

State funded Training and Mindfulness Missions:

Preservation associations and supporters progressively perceive the crucial job of state funded schooling and mindfulness crusades in forming moral contemplations. These drives intend to illuminate the general population about the difficulties looked by lions, the outcomes of deceptive practices, and the aggregate liability to secure and protect these famous species.

4. **Moving Ideal models in Zoos and Hostage Offices:**

Accentuation on Normal Ways of behaving:

Zoos and hostage offices are rethinking their way to deal with creature care, with a developing accentuation on giving conditions that permit to the outflow of normal ways of behaving. Nooks are intended to reenact the states of the wild, reassuring lions to participate in hunting, investigation, and social associations.

Improvement Projects:

Improvement programs have become vital to hostage lion government assistance, offering upgrades that copy the difficulties and assortment of their regular territories. From puzzle feeders to aroma trails, these projects give mental and actual feeling, decreasing fatigue and stereotypic ways of behaving.

Coordinated effort with Protection Drives:

Zoos and hostage offices progressively team up with preservation drives, adding to rearing projects that focus on hereditary variety and backing the protection of wild populaces. This cooperative methodology means to adjust hostage endeavors to more extensive preservation objectives.

Straightforwardness and Public Responsibility:

The call for better lion government assistance incorporates an interest for straightforwardness and public responsibility from zoos and hostage offices.

Expanded examination from general society and support associations requires open correspondence about administration rehearses, creature government assistance guidelines, and protection commitments.

5. **Worldwide Drives and Arrangements:**
Show on Worldwide Exchange Imperiled Species (Refers to):
Refers to assumes a significant part in managing the global exchange of imperiled species, including lions. Developing mindfulness has prompted conversations inside the system of Refers to on fortifying guidelines to resolve issues, for example, prize hunting and the unlawful exchange lion parts.

Worldwide Alliance Against Natural life Dealing:
The worldwide alliance against natural life dealing unites nations, associations, and people to battle unlawful untamed life exchange. Lions, as focuses of this exchange, benefit from worldwide endeavors pointed toward fortifying policing, punishments, and bringing issues to light about the results of natural life dealing.

Worldwide Large Feline Coalition:
The Worldwide Large Feline Coalition, containing states, preservation associations, and supporters, centers around the protection of enormous feline species, including lions. This cooperative exertion means to address normal difficulties, share best practices, and direction protection techniques on a global scale.

Joined Countries Manageable Advancement Objectives (SDGs):
The Unified Countries' SDGs envelop a scope of targets pertinent to lion government assistance, including objectives connected with life ashore, environment activity, and manageable turn of events. The call for better lion government assistance lines up with these more extensive worldwide targets, accentuating the interconnectedness of ecological and social manageability.

6. **Local area Based Preservation and Conjunction:**
   Engaging Nearby People group:
   Local area based preservation perceives the crucial job of neighborhood networks in lion protection. Engaging people group through instruction, elective occupations, and shared benefits from preservation endeavors cultivates a feeling of responsibility and energizes concurrence with lions.

   Human-Natural life Struggle Moderation:
   Tending to human-natural life struggle is a vital part of better lion government assistance. Drives that utilize non-deadly techniques, for example, resistant to hunter domesticated animals nooks and early admonition frameworks, add to alleviating clashes and advancing tranquil conjunction among lions and neighborhood networks.

   Social Responsiveness and Inclusivity:
   Effective preservation procedures recognize and regard the social qualities and practices of neighborhood networks. Social responsiveness guarantees that preservation endeavors are comprehensive and cooperative, encouraging organizations that focus on both lion government assistance and the prosperity of human populaces.

   Monetary Motivators for Protection:
   The call for better lion government assistance includes investigating financial motivations that line up with protection objectives. Drives, for example, ecotourism, which gives monetary advantages to neighborhood networks, add to the practical concurrence of lions and individuals while advancing the government assistance of both.

7. **Examination and Preservation Science:**
   Conduct Studies and Biological Exploration:
   Progressing investigation into lion conduct and natural elements illuminates preservation procedures. Conduct concentrates on in both imprisonment and the wild give experiences into the

requirements of lions, directing the advancement of compelling administration practices and protection mediations.

Mechanical Advancements for Checking:

Innovative progressions, including GPS following, camera traps, and remote detecting, empower more exact checking of lion populaces and their living spaces. These advancements work with information driven protection choices and upgrade how we might interpret the elements impacting lion government assistance.

Hereditary Variety and Populace Wellbeing:

Hereditary investigations add to the preservation of lion populaces by surveying hereditary variety and wellbeing. This data is significant for overseeing hostage reproducing programs, forestalling inbreeding, and advancing the drawn out reasonability of both hostage and wild lion populaces.

Environmental Change Transformation Systems:

Protection science progressively coordinates environmental change variation procedures to address the effects of natural movements on lion living spaces. Understanding what environmental change means for prey accessibility, water sources, and scene elements illuminates proactive preservation estimates that protect lion government assistance.

8. Instructive Drives and Public Commitment:

Lion Protection Training Projects:

Instructive drives assume an imperative part in bringing issues to light and encouraging a feeling of obligation for lion government assistance. Programs in schools, networks, and online stages teach the general population about the difficulties looked by lions and the significance of preservation endeavors.

Media and Narrative Promotion:

Media, including narratives, films, and online stages, act as strong backers for lion government assistance. Convincing narrating and visual accounts add to the worldwide call for better lion government assistance by contacting different crowds and rousing activity.

Impact of VIP Backing:

VIP advocates utilizing their foundation to support lion government assistance add to the intensification of the call for change. Well known people utilizing their impact assist with pointing out basic issues, assemble assets, and urge their supporters to take part in protection endeavors.

Computer generated Reality and Increased Reality Encounters:

Inventive advances, for example, computer generated reality and expanded reality encounters, offer vivid ways of associating crowds with the existences of lions. These intuitive stages extend public comprehension, summon compassion, and improve the viability of instructive drives.

3.2 Activist movements and public outcry

In the consistently developing scene of social and ecological issues, extremist developments and public clamor act as strong impetuses for cultural change. These developments, frequently powered by enthusiastic people and enhanced through far reaching public commitment, have the ability to shape approaches, challenge standards, and affect extraordinary changes in the shared perspective.

This investigation dives into the elements of dissident developments and the reverberation of public objection, analyzing their jobs, influence, and the systems through which they impact change.

The Force of Grassroots Activism:

Lobbyist developments regularly rise out of the grassroots, mirroring the worries and yearnings of customary individuals. Whether pushing for ecological protection, social liberties, orientation uniformity, or other major problems, grassroots activism engages people to become influencers. It is a demonstration of the conviction that aggregate endeavors, regardless of how little, can touch off huge cultural changes.

Online Entertainment Intensification:

The approach of web-based entertainment has altered the manner in which dissident developments work and build up some forward momentum. Stages like Twitter, Instagram, and Facebook give a worldwide stage to people to share data, prepare support, and enhance their messages. Hashtags, viral missions, and online petitions empower activists to contact different crowds and make a virtual local area of similar people focused on a reason.

Perceivability and Mindfulness:

Public objection frequently comes from an elevated familiarity with treacheries, imbalances, or ecological emergencies. Dissident developments assume a crucial part in carrying these issues to the very front of public cognizance. Through fights, rallies, and online entertainment crusades, activists guarantee that their causes are not consigned to the sidelines however are rather recognized and investigated by the more extensive populace.

Shaking things up:

Lobbyist developments upset the state of affairs by testing laid out standards, prejudicial practices, and abusive frameworks. By declining to acknowledge the predominant request of things, activists brief basic assessments of cultural designs and backer for changes that advance equity, correspondence, and maintainability.

Legitimizing Contradiction:

Public objection fills in as an integral asset for legitimizing dispute. At the point when people on the whole voice their interests and complaints, it challenges authority and requests responsibility. Lobbyist developments make spaces for contradicting voices to be heard, cultivating a culture where it isn't just acknowledged yet embraced as a majority rule right to challenge the common story.

Strategy Promotion and Authoritative Change:

Dissident developments frequently channel their energy into strategy promotion, looking for substantial changes in regulation and administration. Through campaigning, public strain, and vital missions, activists impact policymakers to resolve fundamental issues, establish regulations that safeguard common freedoms, and execute guidelines that defend the climate.

Worldwide Fortitude:

Numerous extremist developments rise above public lines, cultivating a feeling of worldwide fortitude. Issues like environmental change, denials of basic freedoms, and civil rights resound on a global scale, prompting cooperative endeavors that join people and associations around the world. The interconnectedness of worldwide difficulties requests aggregate reactions, and extremist developments act as courses for this unified front.

Change in Corporate Practices:

Public clamor and activism likewise influence corporate practices as purchasers request moral, reasonable, and socially dependable business lead. Organizations confronting public reaction for unscrupulous practices frequently reconsider their procedures, prompting changes in supply chains, work rehearses, and natural arrangements.

Social Change:

Lobbyist developments add to social change by testing instilled biases, predispositions, and unfair practices. Through schooling, mindfulness crusades, and comprehensive narrating, activists encourage social moves that focus on variety, inclusivity, and acknowledgment.

Long haul Social Change:

While the prompt effect of lobbyist developments might be clear in arrangement changes or changes in open opinion, their actual power lies in their capability to catalyze long haul social change. By impacting mentalities, molding stories, and motivating people in the future, dissident developments establish the groundwork for a more evenhanded, just, and maintainable society.

3.3 Shift in zoo and wildlife management philosophies

Throughout the long term, there has been an eminent change in the ways of thinking directing the administration of zoos and untamed life. Conventional practices that focused on show and diversion have advanced into comprehensive methodologies revolved around preservation, instruction, and creature government assistance.

This change mirrors a developing consciousness of the moral obligations intrinsic in focusing on hostage creatures and an acknowledgment of the imperative job zoos play in worldwide preservation endeavors.

All things considered, zoos were principally planned as attractions, displaying fascinating species for public diversion. The accentuation was on making outwardly engaging displays as opposed to tending to the perplexing requirements of the creatures. Be that as it may, a change in perspective started to flourish as' how society might interpret the regular ways of behaving, social designs, and prosperity of creatures extended.

Preservation Driven Approach:

Current zoo the executives ways of thinking focus on protection as a center goal. Zoos currently capability as essential center points for rearing projects, species recuperation drives, and cooperative endeavors to protect jeopardized creatures. The hostage rearing of undermined species inside controlled conditions fills in as a wellbeing net against eradication, contributing essentially to worldwide protection objectives.

Instruction and Mindfulness:

Zoos have become strong instructive stages, planning to encourage an association among guests and the normal world. Interpretive displays, instructive projects, and intelligent encounters are intended to educate people in general about the significance regarding biodiversity, territory protection, and the difficulties confronting natural life. The objective is to move a feeling of stewardship and ecological obligation.

Naturalistic Conditions:

The change in way of thinking is clear in the plan of zoo walled in areas. Present day zoos focus on establishing naturalistic conditions that emulate the creatures' local environments. This approach not just improves the prosperity of the creatures yet in addition gives guests a more valid and enhancing experience. Nooks are intended to energize regular ways of behaving, actual work, and social communications.

Conduct Enhancement and Government assistance:

Creature government assistance is a focal thought in contemporary zoo the executives. Social advancement programs are executed to invigorate the physical and mental prosperity of hostage creatures. This might incorporate the presentation of novel items, food riddles, and valuable open doors for socialization. The attention is on advancing species-fitting ways of behaving and limiting pressure related with bondage.

Research and Logical Commitments:

Zoos effectively take part in logical exploration to propel how we might interpret creature conduct, physiology, and veterinary consideration. Research directed in zoological establishments contributes significant bits of knowledge to both hostage and wild populaces. This information illuminates preservation systems, upgrades veterinary practices, and supports endeavors to safeguard species in their normal natural surroundings.

Cooperation with Protection Associations:

Current zoos progressively team up with protection associations, administrative organizations, and other zoological foundations to pool assets and mastery. These associations reach out past zoo limits, supporting field projects, natural surroundings rebuilding, and local area based protection drives all over the planet.

Change in Guest Assumptions:

Guest assumptions play had a crucial impact in driving the change in zoo ways of thinking. The public currently requests straightforwardness, moral treatment of creatures, and an emphasis on preservation and training. Zoos answering these assumptions upgrade their validity as well as add to a more extensive social shift toward dependable stewardship of the planet.

3.4 Legal and ethical considerations for keeping lions in captivit

Keeping lions in bondage raises critical lawful and moral contemplations that stretch out past the prompt government assistance of the creatures. As strong hunters with complex social designs and conduct needs, lions require unique regard for guarantee their prosperity and protection. Understanding and tending to these contemplations are essential for keeping up with moral norms and lawful consistence in the administration of hostage lion populaces.

Legitimate Systems:

Regulations and guidelines overseeing the keeping of lions in bondage shift universally. Numerous nations have explicit untamed life assurance regulations that address the belonging, rearing, and display of extraordinary creatures, including lions. Consistence with these guidelines is fundamental to forestall unlawful natural life exchange, safeguard public security, and advance mindful creature care. Also, peaceful accords, for example, the Show on Global Exchange Jeopardized Types of Wild Fauna and Greenery (Refers to) control the cross-line exchange of lions and their body parts.

Protection and Rearing Projects:

Hostage lion the executives ought to line up with protection objectives, underlining hereditary variety and the safeguarding of sound populaces. Reproducing projects ought to focus on species preservation over business interests, staying away from rehearses like canned hunting, which has moral ramifications and raises worries about the effect on wild populaces.

Creature Government assistance and Moral Treatment:

Guaranteeing the best expectations of creature government assistance is fundamental. Moral contemplations incorporate giving extensive and advanced conditions that imitate regular environments, offering legitimate veterinary consideration, and advancing social associations. The counteraction of stereotypic ways of behaving, marks of pressure in hostage creatures, is a vital moral concern.

Training and Public Mindfulness:

Zoos and offices lodging hostage lions should focus on training and public mindfulness. Moral contemplations reach out to drawing in guests in finding out about lions' regular ways of behaving, preservation challenges, and the significance of safeguarding wild living spaces. Straightforward correspondence about the moral standards directing lion the executives rehearses cultivates public trust and energizes capable way of behaving.

Exploration and Observing:

Taking part in logical examination inside hostage lion populaces adds to better grasping their wellbeing, conduct, and propagation. This exploration helps with refining the executives works on, upgrading creature government assistance, and supporting more extensive preservation drives.

Chapter 4

Lions In Transition

The famous picture of a lion, the undisputed lord of the savannah, has been profoundly imbued in our shared perspective. In any case, the truth of lions in the cutting edge time is one of progress, set apart by a mind boggling transaction of difficulties and potential open doors. This far reaching investigation digs into the complex elements of the ongoing status of lions — both in the wild and in bondage. From the dangers looked by wild populaces to the moral contemplations encompassing bondage, and the developing job of protection endeavors, this story unfurls the tale of lions exploring the complexities of an influencing world.

1. **Wild Lions: Preservation Difficulties and Protection Drives Living space Misfortune and Discontinuity:**
   The first test defying wild lions is the misfortune and discontinuity of their normal living spaces. Quick human populace development, extension of horticulture, and infrastructural improvement have infringed upon lion regions, prompting expanded struggle among people and lions.

Human-Natural life Struggle:

As human exercises infringe on lion living spaces, examples of human-untamed life struggle increase. Lions going after domesticated animals trigger retaliatory killings, representing a critical danger to wild populaces. Tending to this contention requires inventive procedures that balance the necessities of nearby networks with the preservation objectives for lions.

Poaching and Unlawful Exchange:

Poaching for lion parts, driven by conventional convictions and business interests, stays a relentless danger. The unlawful exchange lion bones, skins, and other body parts adds to the downfall of lion populaces. Hostile to poaching endeavors and global cooperation are significant in fighting this unlawful exchange.

Environmental Change and Biological Effect:

Environmental change represents a developing danger to the biological systems that lions occupy. Changes in atmospheric conditions, adjusted prey accessibility, and changes in water sources influence the fragile equilibrium of the savannah. Protection methodologies should consolidate environment flexibility to guarantee the drawn out endurance of lions and their biological systems.

Preservation Methodologies and Examples of overcoming adversity:

In spite of the difficulties, various protection drives are endeavoring to shield wild lion populaces. Contextual investigations of fruitful protection endeavors, for example, local area based projects, movement projects, and territory reclamation, delineate the potential for positive results when networks, state run administrations, and progressives work together.

2. **Hostage Lions: Morals, Government assistance, and the Eventual fate of Zoos**

   Development of Zoos and Natural life Nooks:

   The job of zoos and untamed life nooks has gone through

a significant development. When essentially centered around display and diversion, present day zoos focus on preservation, instruction, and creature government assistance. The progress mirrors a more profound comprehension of the necessities of hostage creatures and the moral obligations related with their consideration.

Moral Contemplations in Hostage Reproducing:

The reproducing of lions in imprisonment has been a subject of moral examination, especially with regards to business interests, for example, prize hunting and the outlandish pet exchange. Inspecting the moral components of hostage rearing includes assessing reproducing rehearses, the effect on hereditary variety, and the commitment to preservation objectives.

Conduct Enhancement and Government assistance:

Upgrading the government assistance of hostage lions is a key thought. Conduct enhancement programs, intended to invigorate normal ways of behaving and forestall stereotypic exercises, add to the physical and mental prosperity of hostage lions. Establishing conditions that reflect the states of the wild is vital to advancing a more excellent of life for these creatures.

Discussions Encompassing Canned Hunting:

The act of canned hunting, where lions are reproduced in imprisonment to be pursued in bound spaces, has ignited critical contention. Moral worries, protection suggestions, and the effect on wild populaces are basic contemplations in assessing the morals of this training and upholding for its discontinuance.

Public Discernment and Training:

Public impression of zoos and hostage offices assumes an essential part in forming moral contemplations. Instructive drives that encourage a comprehension of the intricacies of hostage lion the executives, the significance of protection, and the moral issues included add to informed public talk.

3. **Figuring out Lion Conduct: Bits of knowledge from the Wild and Bondage**

Normal Territory and Conduct of Wild Lions:

Wild lions show complex social designs, agreeable hunting ways of behaving, and unmistakable regional elements. An investigation of their regular territory gives bits of knowledge into the intricacies of their way of behaving, accentuating the requirement for preservation systems that regard and safeguard these normal ways of behaving.

Effect of Imprisonment on Lion Conduct:

The change from the wild to imprisonment presents a large group of difficulties that influence lion conduct. Understanding the mental and actual impacts of imprisonment is fundamental for executing the board rehearses that focus on the government assistance of hostage lions. Perceptions from both wild and hostage settings add to an extensive comprehension of lion conduct.

Mental and Actual Impacts of Nook Life:

Life in imprisonment can significantly affect the mental and actual prosperity of lions. From the improvement of stereotypic ways of behaving to the difficulties of keeping a sound social design, investigating the outcomes of nook life reveals insight into the intricacies of overseeing lions in bondage.

Logical Examinations on Hostage Lion Conduct:

Logical exploration assumes a crucial part in disentangling the complexities of lion conduct in bondage. Social examinations, physiological evaluations, and mental exploration add to the group of information illuminating administration rehearses. Analyzing the discoveries of logical examinations gives significant experiences into the versatile methodologies and difficulties looked by hostage lions.

4. **Difficulties and Reactions of Keeping Lions in Fenced in areas Institutional Difficulties:**

Zoos and hostage offices experience institutional difficulties going from monetary limitations to the board rehearses. Adjusting the requirement for income age with moral contemplations and preservation objectives presents inborn difficulties that request imaginative arrangements.

Social and Legitimate Reactions:

Social view of creature use and imprisonment change broadly, prompting legitimate and social reactions. The moral elements of practices like creature exhibitions, communications, and reproducing for business objects are subjects of lawful examination and cultural discussion.

Basic entitlements and Activism:

The backing for basic entitlements and the moral treatment of creatures has acquired unmistakable quality, prompting expanded investigation of zoos and hostage offices. Extremist developments and public objection have affected popular assessment and, at times, provoked changes in the administration practices of hostage lions.

5. **Developing Consciousness of the Requirement for Better Lion Government assistance**

Public Mindfulness and Backfire:

Developing attention to the difficulties looked by lions in bondage has ignited public reaction against rehearses apparent as deceptive or negative to creature government assistance. Web-based entertainment stages and expanded network have worked with the dispersal of data, prompting elevated public mindfulness and calls for change.

Development of Zoos and Natural life The board Methods of reasoning:

The development of zoo and untamed life the executives ways of thinking mirrors a more extensive change in cultural perspectives toward creature government assistance, preservation, and moral contemplations. From protection driven ways to deal with underlining naturalistic conditions and conduct improvement, the changing methods of reasoning highlight a pledge to working on the government assistance of hostage lions.

Lawful and Moral Contemplations:

Lawful structures administering the keeping of lions in bondage and the moral contemplations related with hostage reproducing, creature government assistance, and protection commitments are key to guaranteeing dependable administration rehearses. Sticking to these contemplations is indispensable for keeping up with the authenticity of hostage offices and encouraging public trust.

Extremist Developments and Public Clamor:

Extremist developments and public clamor act as impetuses for cultural change, affecting general assessment, approaches, and institutional practices. The force of grassroots activism, enhanced through web-based entertainment and public mindfulness crusades, adds to the developing energy for better lion government assistance and moral administration.

6. **Lions On the move: The Call for Change**

   Adjusting to Contemporary Difficulties:

   The call for change keeps on advancing as contemporary difficulties arise. Issues like man-made brainpower morals, bioethics, and the moral ramifications of mechanical progressions require continuous transformation in promotion and cultural reactions.

   The Job of Schooling:

   Schooling fills in as an impetus for change by cultivating decisive reasoning, sympathy, and a feeling of social obligation. Educational plans that address assorted viewpoints, authentic shameful acts, and worldwide difficulties add to making educated and engaged people.

   Youth-Drove Developments:

   Youth-drove developments, driven by enthusiasm and a need to get a move on, have arisen as powerful influencers. From environment strikes to civil rights promotion, youthful activists assume a pivotal part in molding the story and driving cultural change.

The Call for Fundamental Change:
Past resolving individual issues, the call for change progressively stresses the requirement for foundational changes. Developments advocate for rebuilding monetary frameworks, rethinking administration, and destroying institutional boundaries to make all the more and practical social orders.

7. **Developing Attention to the Requirement for Better Lion Government assistance**

Grassroots Activism and Public Clamor:
The developing attention to the requirement for better lion government assistance is intently attached to grassroots activism and public objection. People, associations, and networks are progressively vocal in requesting moral treatment, preservation centered administration, and straightforwardness in the acts of zoos and hostage offices.

Worldwide Endeavors and Cooperative Drives:
The call for better lion government assistance isn't restricted to explicit locales yet resounds universally. Cooperative drives, like the Worldwide Large Feline Coalition and Joined Countries Supportable Advancement Objectives, accentuate the interconnectedness of worldwide endeavors in guaranteeing the prosperity of lions and other huge feline species.

Morals of Preservation Practices:
The moral contemplations encompassing protection works on, including hostage rearing, renewed introduction projects, and natural surroundings conservation, are indispensable to the call for better lion government assistance. Finding some kind of harmony between protection goals and moral guidelines is fundamental for the drawn out progress of preservation drives.

Instructive Missions and Media Support:
Instructive missions and media support assume critical parts in enhancing the call for better lion government assistance. Narratives, online stages, and augmented reality encounters add to public grasping,

compassion, and informed navigation with respect to the moral treatment of lions in both imprisonment and nature.

4.1 Collaborations between zoos, conservation organizations, and wildlife sanctuaries

In the worldwide work to moderate biodiversity and safeguard imperiled species, cooperative organizations assume a crucial part. Zoos, preservation associations, and untamed life safe-havens structure a powerful group of three that synergizes their mastery, assets, and shared obligation to untamed life protection. This exhaustive investigation digs into the meaning of coordinated efforts inside this set of three, analyzing the assorted manners by which these establishments unite to address preservation challenges, advance training, and add to the prosperity of our planet's valuable untamed life.

1. **Zoos: Preservation Past Displays**

   Advancement of Zoos as Preservation Focuses:

   Zoos have gone through a significant change, developing from simple exhibitors of extraordinary creatures to dynamic members in preservation endeavors. Current zoos focus on not just the consideration and government assistance of their occupants yet additionally take part in rearing projects, research drives, and state funded training to add to the conservation of jeopardized species.

   Job in Hostage Reproducing Projects:

   Zoos, with their controlled surroundings and veterinary mastery, assume an essential part in hostage rearing projects. These projects center around species that face impending dangers in the wild, expecting to lay out hereditarily suitable populaces that might possibly be once again introduced into their normal territories.

   Protection Schooling and Public Mindfulness:

   Schooling is a foundation of the cutting edge zoo's central goal. By offering interpretive shows, directed visits, and intelligent projects, zoos raise public mindfulness about the significance of biodiversity, the dangers confronting untamed life, and the job people can play in preservation. This instructive effort encourages a feeling of obligation and ecological stewardship among guests.

2. **Protection Associations: Promoters for Worldwide Safeguarding**

Examination and Support:

Protection associations work on a worldwide scale, leading examination, upholding for strategy changes, and carrying out on-the-ground preservation drives. These associations address general issues, for example, natural surroundings misfortune, environmental change, and unlawful untamed life exchange. Their work is fundamental for making a practical future for untamed life.

Cooperative Protection Arranging:

Preservation associations work together with different partners, including legislatures, neighborhood networks, and other non-administrative associations. These cooperative endeavors include the improvement of key preservation designs that think about the necessities of both untamed life and human populaces. By cultivating associations, protection associations augment their effect and viability.

Financing for Protection Ventures:

Monetary help is pivotal for the outcome of protection projects. Preservation associations frequently go about as financing bodies, giving awards and assets to zoos, safe-havens, and on-the-ground projects. These assets support research, environment reclamation, against poaching endeavors, and different drives pointed toward safeguarding natural life.

3. **Untamed life Safe-havens: Asylums for Saved and Restored Creatures**

Salvage and Recovery:

Untamed life safe-havens act as shelters for creatures that have been protected from different circumstances, including unlawful dealing, natural surroundings annihilation, or wounds in nature.

These safe-havens give a space to restoration, permitting creatures to recuperate truly and mentally before likely delivery or super durable home.

Advancing Normal Ways of behaving:

Safe-havens focus on establishing conditions that emulate the normal environments of their occupants. This center permits safeguarded creatures to communicate regular ways of behaving, structure social securities, and experience a personal satisfaction that may be compromised in different settings. Safe-havens assume a basic part in giving lifetime care to creatures that can't be once again introduced into nature.

Instructive Drives:

Like zoos, natural life asylums take part in instructive drives. Guests are frequently given directed visits, instructive projects, and potential chances to find out about the accounts of individual creatures and the more extensive protection challenges they address. Safe-havens add to bringing issues to light and cultivating sympathy towards untamed life.

4. **Cooperative energies in real life: Cooperative Drives Protection Reproducing and Delivery Projects:**

Cooperative endeavors between zoos, preservation associations, and asylums frequently center around protection rearing projects. Zoos give mastery in creature cultivation and veterinary consideration, preservation associations contribute logical examination and promotion, while safe-havens might assume a part in the arrival of restored creatures.

Environment Reclamation and Security:

The set of three works together on environment reclamation and security projects. Protection associations lead top to bottom examination on basic environments, zoos contribute assets and mastery for in-situ preservation, and asylums may uphold the restoration and arrival of creatures into reestablished territories.

Local area Commitment and Manageable Practices:

Tending to human-natural life struggle and advancing maintainable practices inside neighborhood networks are key parts of cooperative drives. Protection associations work with networks to foster preservation cordial occupations, while zoos and safe-havens contribute by cultivating associations among guests and the significance of worldwide protection endeavors.

Transboundary Preservation:

Numerous species have ranges that length various nations, requiring cross-line coordinated efforts. The set of three cooperates to lay out transboundary preservation drives, utilizing assets and mastery to address dangers that rise above public boundaries.

5. **Difficulties and Contemplations in Coordinated efforts**

Varying Methods of reasoning and Goals:

Regardless of shared protection objectives, zoos, preservation associations, and asylums may have varying methods of reasoning and targets.

Zoos might confront analysis in regards to their job in hostage rearing, while safe-havens might focus on the salvage and care of individual creatures over more extensive preservation objectives. Adjusting these shifted points of view can challenge.

Asset Designation and Financing:

Asset designation and subsidizing are lasting difficulties in protection endeavors. While protection associations might get awards and gifts, zoos and safe-havens might confront monetary requirements. Joint efforts should explore these difficulties to guarantee that assets are dispersed actually and straightforwardly.

Correspondence and Public Discernment:

Successful correspondence is significant in cooperative undertakings. Public impression of zoos, preservation associations, and asylums can influence their capacity to accumulate support. Straightforward correspondence about cooperative drives, their effect, and the common obligation to preservation is fundamental for building public trust.

Strategic Intricacies:

The strategic intricacies of cooperative tasks, particularly those traversing different topographical areas, can plague. Coordination, correspondence, and the foundation of clear conventions are important to beat strategic difficulties and guarantee the outcome of joint drives.

6. **Examples of overcoming adversity and Effect of Coordinated efforts**

Renewed introduction Achievement:

Cooperative endeavors have prompted fruitful renewed introduction programs. Species like the California condor, dark footed ferret, and different primate species have profited from hostage reproducing and renewed introduction drives including zoos, protection associations, and safe-havens.

Local area Drove Protection:

Cooperative drives that focus on local area commitment have yielded positive results. Projects that include neighborhood networks in preservation arranging, manageable practices, and untamed life checking contribute not exclusively to the security of biodiversity yet additionally to the prosperity of human populaces.

Worldwide Backing and Strategy Change:

Cooperative support endeavors have added to worldwide strategy changes. The set of three's joint drives, upheld by research, public mindfulness crusades, and vital associations, have affected approaches connected with untamed life assurance, territory safeguarding, and hostile to poaching measures at both public and worldwide levels.

Instructive Effect:

Cooperative instructive drives lastingly affect public mindfulness. Zoos, protection associations, and asylums cooperating on instructive projects add to an educated and drew openly. This mindfulness, thusly, upholds more extensive preservation objectives and advances a culture of capable stewardship.

4.2 Innovative approaches to create savanna-like environments for captive lions

Making a living space that reflects the common habitat of wild creatures is essential for their physical and mental prosperity. For hostage lions, the test lies in giving a climate that looks like the immense savannas of Africa, where they would wander unreservedly in nature. Imaginative methodologies have arisen inside the domain of zoo plan and creature farming to address this test, expecting to upgrade the personal satisfaction for hostage lions by imitating key components of their normal territory. This investigation dives into a portion of the imaginative methodologies and innovations utilized to establish savanna-like conditions for hostage lions.

1. **Scene Engineering and Plan:**
   Territory Replication:
   Scene engineers and zoo originators utilize territory replication procedures to mirror the undulating scenes of the savanna. By consolidating slopes, slants, and rough outcrops into the nook plan, hostage lions are given fluctuated territory that empowers regular ways of behaving like climbing, running, and reviewing their environmental factors.

   Regular Vegetation and Greenery:
   The decision of vegetation inside the walled in area is critical. Inventive methodologies include choosing plant species local to the lions' normal environment, making a real savanna biome. This not just improves the visual allure of the fenced in area yet in addition fills in as a significant component for the lions to connect with, giving chances to stowing away, aroma stamping, and regional ways of behaving.

   Water Highlights and Fake Waterholes:
   In the wild, lions are attracted to water hotspots for drinking and chilling. Hostage conditions integrate fake water highlights, like lakes or streams, to reproduce this part of the savanna.

These waterholes act as central focuses for the lions, empowering normal ways of behaving and giving an outwardly improving component to the nook.

2. **Mechanical Improvements:**
Increased Reality and Virtual Improvement:
Mechanical developments have presented increased reality and virtual advancement encounters for hostage lions. Projection frameworks or advanced screens can show moving pictures of savanna scenes, prey creatures, or in any event, changing weather conditions. This unique type of improvement invigorates the lions' detects, giving mental excitement and copying the eccentricism of nature.

Environment Control and Counterfeit Sky:
Establishing a savanna-like climate includes repeating the actual elements as well as thinking about the environment. Creative fenced in areas consolidate environment control frameworks that emulate the temperature and weather patterns of the normal territory. Furthermore, counterfeit bay windows or boards are utilized to reproduce the changing examples of the sky, including dawn and nightfall, adding to a more vivid encounter for the lions.

3. **Conduct Enhancement and Intelligent Components:**
Tangible Enhancement and Fragrance Trails:
Savannas are wealthy in aromas, and repeating this olfactory experience is critical for hostage lions. Social enhancement programs present aroma trails utilizing normal smells from plants, prey creatures, or significantly different lions. This invigorates the lions' feeling of smell, empowering exploratory way of behaving and giving a tangible rich climate.

Intelligent Feeders and Puzzle Toys:
Imitating the test of chasing after food in the wild, creative feeders and puzzle toys are presented in bondage. These gadgets support critical thinking ways of behaving, active work, and the normal

savage impulses of lions. Setting food decisively inside the nook advances mental feeling and actual commitment.

4. **Social Elements and Gathering Cooperation:**
Multi-Species Fenced in areas and Social Combination:
Advancements in walled in area configuration investigate the chance of establishing multi-species conditions. Presenting viable species inside a similar nook can reproduce the perplexing social elements saw in nature. This approach enhances the climate for lions as well as encourages regular collaborations between various species, adding to a more powerful and different biological system inside imprisonment.

Dynamic Nook Designs:
The utilization of dynamic nook designs considers occasional changes in the format and highlights of the fenced in area. This development forestalls adjustment, keeping the climate novel and connecting with for the lions. Pivoting or changing components like shakes, logs, or raised stages guarantees that the lions experience new difficulties and amazing open doors for investigation.

5. **Research and Nonstop Improvement:**
Observational Exploration and Conduct Studies:
Progressing research and conduct studies are basic to the outcome of imaginative methodologies. Noticing the lions' reactions to various components inside the savanna-like climate gives significant bits of knowledge. This exploration illuminates changes and upgrades to walled in area configuration, guaranteeing that the hostage climate keeps on advancing in light of the particular necessities and inclinations of the lions.

Input Circles and Guest Collaboration:
Guest collaboration can be incorporated into the criticism circle for consistent improvement. Perceptions of lion conduct, guest criticism, and the adequacy of advancement techniques add to an iterative interaction. This cooperative methodology includes general society in the prosperity of hostage lions and encourages

a feeling of shared liability regarding protection and creature government assistance.

6. **Challenges and Moral Contemplations:**

Offsetting Legitimacy with Security:
Finding some kind of harmony between establishing a genuine savanna-like climate and guaranteeing the security of the two lions and guests is an essential test. Developments should consider potential dangers related with normal highlights, for example, water bodies or complex landscape, while as yet giving an invigorating and drawing in climate.

Space Constraints in Bondage:
While endeavors are made to duplicate normal natural surroundings, the space impediments innate in bondage present difficulties. Establishing broad savanna-like conditions inside bound spaces might challenge. Advancements need to upgrade accessible space to give significant and different encounters to hostage lions.

Social and Lawful Contemplations:
Social discernments and lawful structures can impact the practicality and execution of inventive methodologies. Cooperative endeavors should explore social perspectives toward creature bondage, guaranteeing that advancements line up with moral principles and legitimate prerequisites.

4.3 Benefits observed in lions after transitioning to more natural settings

The change from traditional hostage conditions to additional naturalistic settings has yielded significant advantages for lions under human consideration. This shift mirrors a comprehension of the intricate necessities of these dominant hunters and recognizes the significance of establishing conditions that impersonate their normal territories. Perceptions and studies following such changes have revealed a scope of positive changes in the way of behaving, wellbeing, and generally speaking prosperity of hostage lions. This investigation dives into the prominent advantages saw in lions subsequent to progressing to additional normal settings.

1. **Upgraded Actual Wellbeing and Wellness:**
   Expanded Active work:
   Lions in naturalistic settings show more elevated levels of actual work contrasted with those in conventional fenced in areas. The incorporation of shifted landscape, like shakes and raised stages, invigorates normal ways of behaving like climbing and investigating. This expanded development adds to further developed muscle tone, cardiovascular wellbeing, and in general actual wellness.
   Valuable open doors for Hunting Reproductions:
   Repeating components of the savanna climate considers the presentation of hunting reenactments. Enhancement exercises that include concealing food, utilizing puzzle feeders, or putting prey-scented objects animate the lions' savage impulses. Taking part in these exercises gives mental feeling and energizes critical thinking, adding to the general wellbeing and imperativeness of the creatures.

2. **Mental Excitement and Mental Improvement:**
   Social Variety and Regular Ways of behaving:
   Lions in regular settings show a more different scope of ways of behaving intelligent of their wild partners. From following and jumping to social communications and regional ways of behaving, the naturalistic climate gives a material to the declaration of a more extensive collection of ways of behaving. This social variety adds to mental feeling and forestalls stereotypic ways of behaving related with pressure and fatigue.
   Critical thinking and Mental Difficulties:
   The presentation of components that energize critical thinking, for example, puzzle feeders and secret food sources, presents mental difficulties for hostage lions. Participating in exercises that require thought and technique upgrades their mental capacities.

Perceptions show that lions in additional regular settings show expanded interest and flexibility, exhibiting an uplifted degree of mental commitment.

3. **Social Association and Collective vibes:**
Arrangement of Social Bonds:

Lions are social creatures that blossom with collaborations with conspecifics. In naturalistic settings that consider bunch living, lions structure social bonds, take part in common preparing, and display agreeable ways of behaving. These social collaborations add to the general prosperity of the people and cultivate a more enhanced and dynamic social construction.

Order and Regular Overall vibes:

The change to regular settings works with the foundation of orders and normal overall vibes inside lion prides. Perceptions uncover that the presence of various people in a gathering considers the outflow of complicated social ways of behaving, including play, correspondence, and helpful hunting techniques. This mirrors the mind boggling social designs saw in nature.

4. **Worked on Conceptive Achievement:**
Positive Effect on Rearing Projects:

Naturalistic conditions meaningfully affect hostage rearing projects for lions. The decrease of pressure related with additional bound spaces, joined with the arrangement of appropriate circumstances for romance and mating ways of behaving, adds to expanded conceptive achievement. Fruitful rearing projects are essential for keeping up with hereditary variety and the drawn out manageability of hostage populaces.

Upgraded Maternal Consideration and Fledgling Raising:

Lions in additional normal settings frequently show improved maternal consideration ways of behaving. The accessibility of separated regions for fledgling raising and the regular elements of a pride add to a strong climate for fruitful proliferation. The whelps, thus, benefit from a more improved childhood, mastering fundamental abilities and ways of behaving through perception and connection with the pride.

5. **Positive Effect on Guest Schooling:**
Instructive Open doors for Guests:
Naturalistic settings give improved open doors to guest instruction. Guests can notice lions participated in a scope of normal ways of behaving, acquiring bits of knowledge into the intricacies of their social designs, hunting procedures, and everyday schedules. This experiential learning cultivates a more profound comprehension of the species and advances a more noteworthy appreciation for the preservation challenges they face in nature.

Promotion for Protection and Living space Safeguarding:
Noticing lions in additional normal settings frequently fills in as a strong support device for protection and living space conservation. Zoos and untamed life offices can utilize these conditions to impart the significance of safeguarding the lions' normal territories, bringing issues to light about the difficulties looked by wild populaces, and moving aggregate activity for protection.

6. **Progressing Exploration and Transformation:**

Ceaseless Observing and Exploration:
The advantages saw in lions subsequent to progressing to additional normal settings are much of the time subject to continuous examination and checking. Nonstop perception takes into consideration the documentation of conduct changes, wellbeing upgrades, and the general outcome of the progress. This examination adds to the versatile administration of hostage conditions, guaranteeing that changes can be made in light of the developing necessities of the lions.

Illuminating Accepted procedures:
The encounters of lions in additional normal settings add to the improvement of best practices in hostage creature the board. Experiences acquired from fruitful changes educate the plan regarding future fenced in areas, the advancement of enhancement programs, and the

foundation of rules for establishing conditions that focus on the prosperity of hostage lions.

Chapter 5

Challenges And Solutions

Contemporary society is set apart by a horde of difficulties that range across different spaces, from innovation and medical care to instruction and ecological manageability. These difficulties frequently arise because of cultural, financial, or mechanical headways, requesting inventive answers for guarantee the prosperity and progress of social orders. This investigation dives into key difficulties looked by contemporary society and investigates expected answers for address these complicated issues.

1. **Innovative Difficulties:**
   Network protection Dangers:
   As innovation propels, the gamble of digital dangers keeps on heightening. The interconnected idea of advanced frameworks makes them powerless to hacking, information breaks, and other pernicious exercises.
   Arrangement: Executing strong network protection measures, including encryption, multifaceted confirmation, and ordinary security reviews, is fundamental. Furthermore, public mindfulness and instruction on safe internet based practices can assist

with moderating the dangers.

Protection Concerns:

The assortment and utilization of individual information by innovation organizations raise worries about protection encroachment. Issues, for example, information breaks and the abuse of individual data have become pervasive.

Arrangement: Fortifying information insurance guidelines, cultivating straightforward information rehearses, and engaging people with more noteworthy command over their information through protection settings are basic strides toward tending to security concerns.

Advanced Disparity:

Not every person has equivalent admittance to computerized innovations, prompting an advanced separation. This hole intensifies existing financial imbalances and cutoff points open doors for those without admittance to advanced assets.

Arrangement: Advancing computerized education programs, extending web foundation in underserved regions, and giving reasonable admittance to innovation can assist with connecting the advanced separation.

2. **Medical care Difficulties:**

Worldwide Wellbeing Emergencies:

Occasions like pandemics present huge difficulties to worldwide medical services frameworks, overpowering clinical offices, and featuring the requirement for facilitated global reactions.

Arrangement: Reinforcing worldwide wellbeing framework, putting resources into early recognition frameworks, and encouraging global joint effort in innovative work are essential for compelling reaction to wellbeing emergencies.

Emotional wellness Issues:

The commonness of psychological wellness issues has risen, exacerbated by cultural stressors, social detachment, and the disgrace encompassing emotional well-being.

Arrangement: Advancing psychological well-being mindfulness, growing admittance to psychological wellness administrations, and cultivating a steady and comprehensive cultural climate can add to tending to emotional wellness challenges.

Maturing Populace:

Numerous social orders are confronting the difficulties related with a maturing populace, including expanded medical services requests and the requirement for senior consideration administrations.

Arrangement: Carrying out complete senior consideration programs, putting resources into medical services labor force preparing, and empowering research on maturing related illnesses are fundamental parts of tending to the difficulties presented by a maturing populace.

3. **Instructive Difficulties:**

Admittance to Quality Training:

Abberations in admittance to quality schooling persevere, with underestimated networks frequently confronting restricted assets and instructive open doors.

Arrangement: Executing comprehensive instructive approaches, giving assets to oppressed schools, and utilizing innovation for remote learning can assist with further developing admittance to quality training.

Mechanical Joining in Training:

While innovation offers extraordinary conceivable outcomes in schooling, the combination of computerized devices faces difficulties, for example, an absence of foundation, educator preparing, and impartial access.

Arrangement: Putting resources into instructive innovation framework, giving educator preparing programs, and guaranteeing fair admittance to advanced assets are imperative for effective mechanical reconciliation in training.

4. **Natural Difficulties:**

Environmental Change:

Environmental change presents one of the main dangers to the planet, with climbing temperatures, outrageous climate occasions, and natural debasement.

Arrangement: Carrying out supportable works on, progressing to environmentally friendly power sources, and encouraging worldwide participation to diminish ozone depleting substance discharges are basic moves toward tending to environmental change.

Biodiversity Misfortune:

The deficiency of biodiversity because of living space obliteration, contamination, and environmental change has flowing impacts on biological systems and postures dangers to human prosperity.

Arrangement: Executing preservation drives, safeguarding regular environments, and advancing reasonable land-use rehearses are fundamental for saving biodiversity.

Squander The executives:

The rising age of waste, including plastic contamination, presents difficulties for squander the executives and ecological maintainability.

Arrangement: Taking on roundabout economy standards, advancing reusing projects, and lessening single-utilize plastic utilization can add to compelling waste administration.

5. **Social Difficulties:**

Imbalance and Civil rights:

Steady financial imbalances, segregation, and social treacheries stay unavoidable issues in contemporary society.

Arrangement: Carrying out approaches that address fundamental imbalances, advancing variety and incorporation, and cultivating social mindfulness and sympathy are urgent for accomplishing civil rights.

Political Polarization:

Disruptive political philosophies and polarization add to social dissension, thwarting compelling administration and coordinated effort.

Arrangement: Empowering open exchange, advancing media education, and cultivating a culture of give and take and coordinated effort can assist with moderating political polarization.

Relocation and Removal:

Constrained relocation because of contention, ecological catastrophes, and financial elements presents difficulties for both uprooted populaces and host networks.

Arrangement: Carrying out others conscious movement approaches, tending to main drivers of removal, and advancing worldwide participation in displaced person resettlement are fundamental parts of tending to relocation challenges.

6. **Monetary Difficulties:**

Pay Imbalance:

Augmenting pay holes between the rich and poor add to social turmoil and cutoff monetary open doors for minimized populaces.

Arrangement: Carrying out moderate tax collection, advancing comprehensive monetary strategies, and putting resources into training and labor force advancement can assist with tending to pay disparity.

Robotization and Occupation Uprooting:

Progressions in innovation, including mechanization and man-made reasoning, raise worries about work uprooting and the requirement for labor force variation.

Arrangement: Putting resources into reskilling and upskilling programs, encouraging business, and creating strategies that help a smooth change notwithstanding mechanization can relieve the effects of occupation dislodging.

5.1 Obstacles faced during the transition process

The course of progress, whether in private life, profession, or cultural changes, is in many cases set apart by various hindrances that people and networks should explore. These obstacles can emerge from different sources, including outer conditions, inner elements, and unanticipated difficulties. In this investigation, we dive into the bunch deterrents experienced during progress processes and their effect on people and social orders.

Protection from Change:

One of the most widely recognized snags during progress is protection from change. Individuals, commonly, will more often than not avoid disturbances to laid out schedules and recognizable conditions. Whether in authoritative rebuilding or individual life altering events, the opposition can appear at both individual and aggregate levels. Beating this obstruction requires viable correspondence, straightforwardness, and a very much planned change the executives methodology.

Vulnerability and Apprehension about the Unexplored world:

Progress frequently introduces a time of vulnerability, and the feeling of dread toward the obscure can incapacitate. People might wonder whether or not to embrace change because of worries about possible dangers and the eccentric results related with another stage. Building versatility and offering help systems can assist people with standing up to these feelings of dread and settle on informed choices during the change.

Absence of Assets:

Deficient assets, be it monetary, human, or innovative, can hinder the smooth movement of a progress. In authoritative settings, spending plan requirements and restricted labor supply might ruin the execution of new systems. People going through private advances might confront monetary difficulties. Recognizing and tending to asset holes is critical for an effective progress.

Correspondence Breakdowns:

Viable correspondence is a key part for effective changes. Breakdowns in correspondence can prompt disarray, falsehood, and an absence of arrangement among partners. Whether in a corporate consolidation or a cultural shift, cultivating open and straightforward correspondence channels is fundamental to moderate false impressions and construct a common perspective of the progress' goals.

Deficient Preparation:

Foolish advances are inclined to disappointment. Deficient arranging can bring about neglected subtleties, insufficient gamble evaluation, and an absence of possibility measures. Whether it's a venture rollout or an individual life change, fastidious arranging is indispensable. Sufficient time spent in the arranging stage expects difficulties and guarantees a smoother progress direction.

Social and Social Elements:

In cultural changes, social and social elements assume a significant part. Protection from social change, character emergencies, and conflicts of values can arise, thwarting the general progress process. Recognizing and tending to these social subtleties is basic for an amicable change that regards different viewpoints and characters.

Administration Difficulties:

Compelling administration is instrumental in exploring changes effectively. In any case, initiative difficulties like an absence of vision, hesitation, or incapable administration styles can fuel the hardships. Solid authority that cultivates trust, gives direction, and exhibits versatility is fundamental in guiding through the snags intrinsic in any change.

Innovative Interruptions:

In a period set apart by fast mechanical headways, advances are in many cases joined by mechanical disturbances. Consolidating new innovations can present difficulties connected with preparing, incorporation, and possible obstruction from people familiar with conventional strategies. An essential way to deal with mechanical changes is vital for saddle the advantages without causing unjustifiable disturbances.

Lawful and Administrative Obstacles:

Changes, particularly in authoritative or cultural settings, may experience lawful and administrative snags. Exploring complex lawful structures, consistence issues, and administrative necessities can be tedious and asset escalated. Connecting with legitimate specialists and guaranteeing an extensive comprehension of pertinent guidelines is pivotal to stay away from lawful traps during the change.

Mental Effect:

The mental cost of progress ought to be acknowledged with a sober mind. People might wrestle with pressure, nervousness, and a feeling of misfortune during times of huge change. Perceiving the mental effect and giving emotional wellness support is indispensable for the prosperity of those going through change, whether on an individual or cultural level.

Inheritance Frameworks and Attitudes:

Inheritance frameworks and dug in mentalities can block progress during advances. In hierarchical settings, obsolete cycles and protection from new systems can block advancement. Likewise, cultural changes might confront obstruction from people sticking to customary convictions. Conquering these difficulties requires a fragile harmony between saving significant parts of the past and embracing important changes.

Financial Limitations:

Financial contemplations frequently assume a significant part in changes. People and associations the same might confront monetary imperatives that limit their capacity to adjust to new conditions. Creating systems that offset monetary security with the requests of the progress is vital for moderating financial difficulties.

5.2 Addressing concerns related to reintroducing lions to more natural environments

The possibility of once again introducing lions to additional common habitats holds both commitment and difficulties. While the thought plans to reestablish biological equilibrium and upgrade biodiversity, it isn't without critical worries. Addressing these worries is vital to guarantee the outcome of such drives. In this investigation, we dig into the complex parts of once again introducing lions to regular habitats, analyzing biological, cultural, and protection related concerns and proposing techniques to explore them.

Natural Effect:

The renewed introduction of lions to additional regular habitats unavoidably brings up issues about the environmental effect on existing biological systems. Concerns revolve around expected disturbances to prey populaces, changes in vegetation designs, and the general equilibrium of the environment. Leading intensive environmental examinations and effect evaluations preceding renewed introduction is fundamental to comprehend the possible results and carry out measures to relieve any unfavorable impacts.

Prey Populace Elements:

One of the essential biological worries spins around the effect of once again introduced lions on prey populaces. An unmanaged expansion in the lion populace might prompt overhunting of prey species, disturbing the sensitive equilibrium of hunter prey connections. Carrying out extensive checking projects to follow both lion and prey populaces can help in changing administration procedures, like controlled winnowing or movement, to keep a maintainable biological balance.

Human-Natural life Struggle:

The renewed introduction of lions achieves the potential for expanded human-untamed life struggle. As lions recover their regular domains, clashes with neighborhood networks might emerge, particularly in regions where farming and human settlements cross with lion environments. Executing people group commitment programs, laying out successful hunter resistant fencing, and giving remuneration to domesticated animals misfortunes are basic parts of alleviating human-natural life clashes and encouraging conjunction.

Sickness Transmission:

The movement and renewed introduction of lions likewise present dangers of illness transmission, both to neighborhood natural life and homegrown creatures. Sicknesses, for example, canine sickness and ox-like tuberculosis can devastatingly affect populaces. Thorough well-being screening of people before renewed introduction, progressing checking for sickness pervasiveness, and executing quarantine measures are fundamental stages to limit the gamble of illness transmission during and after the renewed introduction process.

Hereditary Variety and Inbreeding:

Little, confined populaces of lions might experience the ill effects of diminished hereditary variety, prompting expanded powerlessness to sicknesses and diminished generally wellness. Once again introducing lions to additional indigenous habitats should think about the hereditary strength of both occupant and once again introduced populaces. Hereditary observing, painstakingly arranged movements, and the foundation of passageways to interface divided environments can assist with keeping up with hereditary variety and forestall inbreeding.

Poaching Dangers:

The unlawful untamed life exchange and poaching exercises represent a critical danger to once again introduced lion populaces. The appeal of important lion parts, like bones and skins, can prompt designated killings. Fortifying enemy of poaching measures, working together with policing, and drawing in nearby networks in protection endeavors can assist with alleviating the dangers presented by poaching and guarantee the drawn out endurance of once again introduced lion populaces.

Living space Appropriateness and Network:

Renewed introduction endeavors should cautiously think about the appropriateness of the picked environments and the availability between these areas. Lacking environment quality or divided scenes can restrict the outcome of renewed introduction drives.

Directing exhaustive territory evaluations, recognizing and addressing likely obstructions to development, and executing natural surroundings rebuilding measures are essential for establishing conditions that can support suitable lion populaces.

The travel industry Effect:

Lions are much of the time a significant draw for untamed life the travel industry, and the renewed introduction of lions to regular habitats can influence existing the travel industry elements. Concerns incorporate likely aggravations to regular ways of behaving, expanded human-natural life collaborations, and the requirement for mindful the travel industry rehearses. Creating and upholding practical the travel industry rules, teaching guests on dependable untamed life seeing, and integrating local area based the travel industry drives can assist with finding some kind of harmony between preservation objectives and the travel industry interests.

Environmental Change Contemplations:

Environmental change adds one more layer of intricacy to the renewed introduction of lions. Modified atmospheric conditions, moving vegetation zones, and changes in prey dispersion can affect the appropriateness of once again introduced living spaces. Environment strong preservation arranging, progressing checking of natural changes, and versatile administration systems are fundamental for address the difficulties presented by environmental change and guarantee the drawn out outcome of renewed introduction endeavors.

Moral Contemplations:

Once again introducing lions to additional regular habitats brings up moral issues connected with human mediation in environments. Some contend that the emphasis ought to be on protecting existing natural surroundings and tending to the main drivers of populace decline instead of falling back on renewed introduction. Participating in straightforward and comprehensive dynamic cycles, including neighborhood networks in preservation arranging, and focusing on the government assistance of individual creatures are fundamental for exploring the moral elements of lion renewed introduction drives.

5.3 The role of technology in monitoring and supporting lions in transition

In the domain of preservation, the coordination of innovation has arisen as a strong partner in checking and supporting lions during momentary stages. The difficulties looked by lion populaces, including environment misfortune, human-natural life struggle, and poaching, require inventive methodologies for successful protection.

This investigation dives into the essential job of innovation in checking and supporting lions as they explore changes, accentuating how progressions in different fields add to their protection and prosperity.

GPS Following and Telemetry:

One of the principal advances driving lion checking is GPS following and telemetry. These frameworks give constant information on the development and conduct of individual lions, offering significant bits of knowledge into their going examples, cooperations, and regional ways of behaving. By outfitting lions with GPS collars, scientists and protectionists can accumulate information from a distance, empowering a far reaching comprehension of their nature and working with informed decision-production during times of progress.

Remote Detecting and Satellite Imaging:

Remote detecting innovations, including satellite imaging, assume a vital part in checking lion environments and scenes. These apparatuses give high-goal pictures that guide in surveying natural surroundings quality, distinguishing possible dangers, and planning land-use changes. Remote detecting is especially significant during momentary stages, permitting protectionists to screen adjustments in vegetation, track territory fracture, and evaluate the effect of ecological changes on lion populaces.

Camera Traps and Mechanized Acknowledgment:

Camera traps furnished with computerized acknowledgment programming have altered untamed life checking. With regards to lion preservation, these gadgets catch pictures and recordings without human presence, offering non-meddlesome bits of knowledge into lion conduct. High level picture acknowledgment calculations can recognize individual lions in light of their extraordinary elements, adding to populace gauges and assisting analysts with following the outcome of renewed introduction endeavors or screen the recuperation of populaces on the move.

Bioacoustic Observing:

Bioacoustic observing includes the utilization of sound-recording gadgets to catch and break down vocalizations of lions and other untamed life. This innovation supports populace appraisals, conduct studies, and the location of trouble calls or expected clashes. During progress stages, bioacoustic observing can give early signs of pressure or changes in friendly elements, permitting preservationists to mediate speedily and address arising difficulties.

Information Examination and Man-made reasoning:

The mix of information investigation and man-made consciousness (simulated intelligence) has improved the productivity of lion observing projects. These innovations interaction huge datasets, distinguishing examples and patterns that could slip through the cracks with customary techniques. Computer based intelligence calculations can examine huge measures of camera trap information, satellite symbolism, and telemetry data, giving important bits of knowledge into lion conduct, wellbeing, and territory inclinations during temporary stages.

Protection Robots:

Protection drones offer an elevated perspective of lion natural surroundings, taking into consideration fast and broad studies. Outfitted with high-goal cameras and sensors, robots can screen immense regions, distinguish likely dangers, and evaluate the viability of protection measures. On the move situations, drones give a financially savvy and time-effective method for getting basic data, working with versatile administration systems because of dynamic natural and environmental changes.

Collar-Mounted Biometric Sensors:

Progressions in biometric sensors have prompted the improvement of collar-mounted gadgets that screen the physiological soundness of lions. These sensors can follow essential signs, for example, pulse, internal heat level, and feelings of anxiety. Checking the prosperity of individual lions during changes is fundamental, and collar-mounted biometric sensors offer a painless method for evaluating their wellbeing, distinguish early indications of trouble, and give ideal veterinary mediation if vital.

Local area Based Checking Applications:

Drawing in nearby networks in lion protection endeavors is essential for progress. Local area based observing applications engage occupants to report lion sightings, episodes of human-untamed life struggle, or indications of poaching. By cultivating a cooperative methodology, these applications work with ideal reactions to arising difficulties and guarantee that the viewpoints and worries of nearby networks are incorporated into protection systems during times of lion change.

Blockchain Innovation for Hostile to Poaching Endeavors:

The battle against poaching is a basic part of lion preservation. Blockchain innovation has been applied to make straightforward and secure frameworks for following and confirming enemy of poaching endeavors.

From observing watch courses to guaranteeing the credibility of held onto natural life items, blockchain upgrades responsibility and diminishes the effect of criminal operations, in this manner shielding lions during changes when they might be especially powerless against poaching dangers.

Expanded Reality (AR) for Training and Mindfulness:

Mechanical advancements stretch out past checking and straightforwardly add to public mindfulness and schooling. Expanded Reality (AR) applications permit clients to encounter virtual experiences with lions, encouraging a feeling of association and sympathy. By instructing the general population about the significance of lion protection and the difficulties they face during changes, AR innovations add to a more extensive comprehension and backing for preservation endeavors.

5.4 Lessons learned from past mistakes and failures

In the embroidered artwork of life, missteps and disappointments are unavoidable strings that add to the rich texture of our encounters. While the close to home sting of disappointment might be significant, the examples gathered from these difficulties frequently act as priceless educators, forming our personality, strength, and future undertakings. This investigation digs into the significant examples gained from previous slip-ups and disappointments, stressing their groundbreaking power in private, proficient, and cultural settings.

Strength and Flexibility:

One of the essential illustrations got from disappointments is the development of strength and versatility. Difficulties force people to face startling difficulties and adjust to evolving conditions. The capacity to quickly return from disappointment, recalibrate procedures, and persist despite difficulty turns into a critical fundamental ability. In self-improvement, versatility is the foundation of exploring life's unavoidable promising and less promising times with beauty and assurance.

Self-Reflection and Self-improvement:

Botches give prolific ground to self-reflection and self-awareness. Disappointment prompts people to inspect their activities, choices, and inspirations with a basic eye. This reflective interaction establishes the groundwork for mindfulness and self-improvement. By recognizing botches, people can distinguish designs, refine their qualities, and diagram a course toward turning out to be better renditions of themselves.

Lowliness and Compassion:

Encountering disappointment encourages modesty by destroying deceptions of strength. Whether in private connections or expert undertakings, mishaps humble people, offering a portion of reality that adds to a more grounded viewpoint. Besides, the sympathy brought into the world from individual disappointments permits people to interface with other people who are confronting comparative difficulties, encouraging a feeling of shared mankind and understanding.

Advancement and Innovativeness:

History is loaded with instances of developments that rose up out of disappointments and slip-ups. The readiness to try, combined with the opportunity to fizzle, is much of the time an impetus for notable revelations. In the expert domain, associations that embrace a culture that endures sensible dangers and gains from disappointment are bound to encourage imagination and development among their groups.

Adherence to Moral Standards:

Disappointments can act as obvious tokens of the significance of moral way of behaving and adherence to standards. Outrages, corporate breakdowns, and individual ruins frequently result from slips in moral judgment. Gaining from these errors builds up the meaning of trust-worthiness, genuineness, and moral direction. People and associations that focus on moral contemplations in their activities are better furnished to explore difficulties with their notorieties flawless.

Compelling Navigation:

Botches, particularly those originating from unfortunate navigation, highlight the requirement for creating successful thinking abilities. Disappointments enlighten the results of surged decisions, insufficient data, or a shortfall of smart thought. The people who gain from their missteps become capable at settling on informed choices, weighing possible results, and taking into account the drawn out ramifications of their decisions.

Affirmation of Mix-ups and Responsibility:

The fortitude to concede missteps and take responsibility is an important example drawn from disappointments. Whether in private connections, administrative roles, or cooperative undertakings, recognizing blunders encourages trust and believability. Pioneers who transparently concede their errors set a strong model, advancing a culture of responsibility and consistent improvement inside their groups.

Tirelessness and Assurance:

Disappointments frequently test a singular's tirelessness and assurance. The way to progress is seldom direct, and mishaps can deter.

Notwithstanding, the individuals who incorporate the examples from disappointments develop a persevering soul. This constancy empowers people to weather conditions storms, conquer impediments, and seek after their objectives with enduring assurance.

Social and Authoritative Learning:

In authoritative settings, gaining from previous slip-ups is crucial for institutional development. Developing a learning society where disappointments are seen as any open doors for development instead of wellsprings of fault encourages consistent learning and variation. Associations that focus on gaining from disappointments are better prepared to develop, adjust to advertise changes, and flourish in powerful conditions.

Adjusting Hazard and Mindfulness:

Previous slip-ups give important bits of knowledge into the fragile harmony among hazard and wariness. While risk-taking is fundamental for progress, foolishness can prompt disappointment. Gaining from botches implies figuring out the subtleties of hazard, going with informed choices, and taking on an essential methodology that limits likely unfortunate results.

Chapter 6

The Impact On Conservation

Preservation remains as a crucial support point in our aggregate liability to protect the planet's biodiversity and environmental equilibrium. Throughout the long term, the effect on protection has gone through huge changes, molded by human exercises, logical progressions, and developing natural difficulties. This exposition investigates the complex components of the effect on protection, diving into verifiable settings, human-incited difficulties, mechanical intercessions, and the future direction of preservation endeavors.

II. Authentic Setting of Protection

The underlying foundations of protection can be followed back to when humankind perceived the need to coincide amicably with the regular world. The nineteenth and mid twentieth hundreds of years saw the rise of protection standards, advocated by figures like John Muir and Theodore Roosevelt. Developments, for example, the foundation of public parks and the arrangement of preservation associations checked essential achievements. This verifiable setting established the groundwork for contemporary preservation practices and set up for continuous endeavors to secure and support the World's biodiversity.

III. Human Exercises and Their Effect on Protection
Environment Obliteration and Discontinuity:

The persistent development of human settlements and modern exercises has brought about far reaching territory annihilation and discontinuity. Urbanization, farming, and framework improvement infringe upon normal natural surroundings, undermining incalculable species. Discontinuity disturbs biological systems, making it provoking for species to track down appropriate favorable places, search for food, and keep up with suitable populaces.

Contamination and Environmental Change:

Human-instigated contamination, including air and water contamination, represents a serious danger to preservation endeavors. The arrival of poisons into the climate, combined with the heightening effect of environmental change, has prompted territory debasement and adjusted biological systems. Protectionists wrestle with the difficulties presented by changing atmospheric conditions, climbing temperatures, and the subsequent changes in the circulation of verdure.

Overexploitation of Regular Assets:

Unreasonable abuse of regular assets, driven by overconsumption and uncontrolled financial exercises, has driven numerous species to the edge of eradication. Overfishing, unlawful logging, and poaching for untamed life exchange devastatingly affect environments and add to the downfall of various species. Finding some kind of harmony between human necessities and the protection of biodiversity stays a basic test.

Intrusive Species and Their Effect:

The presentation of non-local species into environments, whether deliberately or incidentally, has prompted the relocation of native vegetation. Obtrusive species can outcompete local species for assets, upset food networks, and modify the actual texture of environments. Controlling and moderating the effect of obtrusive species has turned into a squeezing worry for protectionists around the world.

IV. Mechanical Mediations in Protection
GPS Following and Telemetry:

Mechanical headways, especially in the domain of following and telemetry, have changed protection rehearses. GPS-empowered GPS beacons permit specialists to screen the developments of natural life progressively, giving important bits of knowledge into relocation examples, conduct, and territory use. This innovation helps with the advancement of informed preservation procedures and works with the security of basic territories.

Remote Detecting and Satellite Imaging:

Remote detecting innovations, for example, satellite imaging, offer an elevated perspective of scenes, empowering progressives to evaluate natural surroundings changes, screen deforestation, and track land-use designs. These instruments add to the improvement of preservation methodologies by giving ideal and precise data about ecological changes for an enormous scope.

Camera Traps and Mechanized Acknowledgment:

Camera traps furnished with robotized acknowledgment programming have become significant instruments for untamed life observing. These gadgets catch pictures and recordings without human presence, considering non-nosy perception of subtle species. Mechanized acknowledgment calculations further upgrade the proficiency of information investigation, empowering specialists to recognize and follow individual creatures for populace review.

Bioacoustic Observing:

Bioacoustic observing includes the utilization of sound-recording gadgets to catch and investigate creature vocalizations. This innovation helps with species ID, populace appraisals, and the checking of untamed life in testing landscapes. Bioacoustic information give urgent data to preservationists attempting to safeguard imperiled species and figure out the elements of biological systems.

Information Examination and Man-made consciousness:

The mix of information examination and man-made brainpower has engaged moderates to process and investigate tremendous datasets effectively. Man-made intelligence calculations can filter through enormous measures of data, recognizing examples, patterns, and relationships that illuminate protection techniques. From anticipating natural life movement courses to surveying the effect of environmental change, information investigation and artificial intelligence upgrade the accuracy and viability of preservation endeavors.

Preservation Robots:

Automated ethereal vehicles, or robots, outfitted with high-goal cameras and sensors, have become essential devices for protectionists. Robots can review huge and blocked off regions, screen natural life populaces, and survey the wellbeing of biological systems. The constant information they give add to informed direction, particularly in preservation drives pointed toward safeguarding jeopardized species and their natural surroundings.

Collar-Mounted Biometric Sensors:

The improvement of choker mounted biometric sensors permits progressives to screen the wellbeing and prosperity of individual creatures in nature. These sensors track essential signs, for example, pulse, internal heat level, and feelings of anxiety, giving experiences into the physiological reactions of creatures to natural changes. This innovation helps with early discovery of medical problems and works with designated mediations for the protection of jeopardized species.

Local area Based Checking Applications:

Tackling the force of local area commitment, progressives have embraced portable applications that empower nearby networks to partake in untamed life observing. These applications permit occupants to report natural life sightings, episodes of poaching, or environment changes. By including networks in protection endeavors, these applications cultivate a feeling of shared liability and advance supportable practices that benefit the two individuals and natural life.

Blockchain Innovation for Against Poaching Endeavors:

The use of blockchain innovation has arisen as a powerful device in the battle against poaching and the unlawful untamed life exchange. Blockchain guarantees straightforward and carefully designed records of against poaching endeavors, from watching exercises to the capture of natural life items. By improving responsibility and diminishing defilement, blockchain innovation adds to the adequacy of against poaching drives.

Increased Reality (AR) for Schooling and Mindfulness:

Expanded Reality (AR) applications have found a spot in preservation schooling and mindfulness crusades. AR permits clients to encounter virtual experiences with untamed life, bringing issues to light about the significance of biodiversity and the difficulties looked by jeopardized species. By utilizing innovation to make vivid instructive encounters, moderates expect to rouse sympathy and encourage a more profound comprehension of the normal world.

V. Difficulties and Future Direction of Protection

Worldwide Joint effort and Strategy Execution:

Regardless of mechanical headways, protection endeavors face difficulties that rise above public limits. Accomplishing significant effect requires improved worldwide joint effort, the execution of hearty global strategies, and a common obligation to resolving squeezing ecological issues. Moderates should explore international intricacies to cultivate aggregate activity for the safeguarding of biodiversity.

Moral Contemplations in Protection Innovation:

The coordination of innovation in protection raises moral contemplations that request cautious examination. Adjusting the advantages of information driven approaches with moral contemplations, for example, protection concerns and the prosperity of observed creatures, is fundamental. Finding some kind of harmony between mechanical advancement and moral standards guarantees that protection rehearses are viable as well as lined up with moral principles.

Local area Contribution and Native Information:

Feasible protection rehearses require the dynamic contribution of nearby networks and the acknowledgment of native information. Drawing in networks in dynamic cycles, regarding customary environmental information, and guaranteeing that protection drives line up with nearby necessities are essential components for the drawn out progress of preservation endeavors.

Environmental Change Transformation and Alleviation:

Environmental change represents an existential danger to biodiversity and intensifies the difficulties looked by protectionists. Methodologies for environmental change variation and moderation should be incorporated into preservation plans. This incorporates the distinguishing proof of environment strong territories, the improvement of systems to safeguard weak species, and backing for worldwide drives to address the main drivers of environmental change.

Subsidizing and Asset Distribution:

Supporting preservation endeavors requires satisfactory subsidizing and asset allotment. States, non-administrative associations, and altruistic substances assume essential parts in supporting preservation drives. Guaranteeing the monetary supportability of preservation projects is fundamental for the proceeded with insurance of biological systems and the protection of biodiversity.

6.1 Contribution of well-adjusted captive lions to global conservation efforts

The discussion encompassing hostage lions and their job in worldwide preservation endeavors is complicated and multi-layered. While the preservation local area has customarily centered around safeguarding species in their regular natural surroundings, composed hostage lions can make huge commitments to more extensive protection objectives. This paper investigates the positive effect that composed hostage lions can have on worldwide protection endeavors, looking at the jobs they play in training, logical examination, hereditary variety conservation, and potential renewed introduction programs.

1. **Instructive Worth of Composed Hostage Lions:**
   Advancing Mindfulness and Understanding:
   Composed hostage lions act as strong instructive apparatuses, encouraging mindfulness and comprehension of these heavenly

animals. Zoos, safe-havens, and natural life parks offer guests the potential chance to notice lions very close, giving an unmistakable association that invigorates interest and sympathy. This first-hand experience adds to a more profound comprehension of lion conduct, nature, and the difficulties they face in nature.

Preservation Informing and Backing:

Hostage lions become diplomats for their wild partners, conveying a protection message that contacts different crowds. Instructive projects at hostage offices can convey the earnestness of safeguarding lions in the wild, bringing issues to light about living space misfortune, poaching, and the significance of protection drives. Thusly, this elevated mindfulness can convert into public help for preservation endeavors internationally.

Supporting Preservation Drives:

All around educated and drew in guests to hostage offices are bound to help preservation drives monetarily and through support. Hostage lions add to raising money endeavors, empowering zoos and asylums to dispense assets to handle projects, hostile to poaching measures, and natural surroundings rebuilding programs. Accordingly, the instructive worth of composed hostage lions stretches out past their actual presence to help worldwide preservation drives effectively.

2. **Logical Exploration Open doors:**

Social Investigations and Ethological Exploration:

Concentrating on the way of behaving of composed hostage lions gives significant experiences into their regular impulses, social designs, and correspondence designs. This exploration is vital for upgrading how we might interpret the species, illuminating protection techniques, and working with the improvement of powerful administration plans for both hostage and wild populaces.

Clinical and Veterinary Exploration:

Hostage lions offer a controlled climate for clinical and veterinary exploration, permitting researchers to concentrate on infections, conceptive physiology, and wellbeing related issues. This exploration has direct applications for wild populaces, adding to the improvement of protection mediations, for example, infection the board and veterinary consideration for nothing running lions confronting wellbeing challenges.

Hereditary Variety Studies:

Keeping up with hereditary variety is a basic part of worldwide preservation endeavors. Hostage lion populaces, oversaw through painstakingly arranged reproducing programs, give an amazing chance to concentrate on hereditary variety, genealogy elements, and potential inbreeding gambles. This information is priceless for planning hereditary administration methodologies that can be applied to wild populaces confronting comparative difficulties.

3. **Hereditary Variety Protection:**

Guaranteeing Sound Populace Elements:

Composed hostage lions add to the protection of hereditary variety by partaking in painstakingly overseen reproducing programs. These projects intend to guarantee solid populace elements, forestall inbreeding, and keep a different genetic supply. By decisively matching lions in light of hereditary contemplations, hostage offices assume a part in protecting the drawn out suitability of the species.

Protection Populaces and Preservation Flexibility:

Hostage lions can act as protection populaces, shielding hereditary variety against the vulnerabilities looked by wild populaces. In case of unanticipated dangers, for example, sickness flare-ups or territory misfortune, very much oversaw hostage populaces can go about as supplies of hereditary variety, giving a likely source to renewed introduction endeavors or species recuperation drives.

Renewed introduction Projects and Hereditary Commitments:

In specific cases, balanced hostage lions might add to renewed introduction programs pointed toward reestablishing populaces in their regular natural surroundings. Via cautiously choosing people with explicit hereditary characteristics helpful for endurance in the wild, hostage offices can improve the outcome of renewed introduction endeavors and support the hereditary strength of declining or divided wild populaces.

4. **Potential for Renewed introduction Projects: Groundwork for Renewed introduction:**

Composed hostage lions, particularly those brought into the world in controlled conditions, can go through specific preparation to foster fundamental abilities to survive expected for renewed introduction into nature. This readiness might incorporate figuring out how to chase, keeping away from hunters, and exploring regular scenes. Such projects improve the probability of effective renewed introduction and transformation to the difficulties of nature.

Tending to Protection Difficulties:

The renewed introduction of hostage lions into painstakingly chose and restored territories tends to different protection challenges. This approach can add to the reclamation of environments, help in controlling prey populaces, and moderate contentions with neighborhood networks. By decisively executing renewed introduction programs, preservationists influence the capability of composed hostage lions to address biological irregular characteristics and backing more extensive protection objectives.

5. **Moral Contemplations and Government assistance Norms:**

Guaranteeing Creature Government assistance:

The commitment of balanced hostage lions to worldwide protection endeavors should be supported by a pledge to the best expectations of creature government assistance. Moral contemplations request that the prosperity of hostage lions is focused on, including satisfactory room, improvement exercises, appropriate veterinary consideration, and conditions that reflect their regular ways of behaving. Finding some kind of harmony between protection goals and creature government assistance is basic for the believability and moral remaining of hostage programs.

Straightforwardness in Hostage The board:

Straightforwardness in the administration of hostage offices is significant for building public trust and gathering support for preservation drives. Moral contemplations incorporate giving clear data about the motivations of hostage programs, the circumstances in which creatures are kept, and the commitments put forth to worldwide protection attempts. Open correspondence cultivates responsibility and guarantees that hostage lions truly add to preservation without undermining their government assistance.

6.2 Role of zoos and sanctuaries in educating the public about lion conservation

Zoos and safe-havens assume a significant part in forming public discernments, encouraging mindfulness, and driving instructive drives zeroed in on lion preservation. As ministers for their wild partners, lions in bondage become amazing assets for conveying the criticalness of saving biodiversity and safeguarding these grand animals. This article dives into the diverse job of zoos and asylums in teaching general society about lion preservation, investigating the instructive methodologies utilized, the effect on guest mindfulness, and the moral contemplations intrinsic in these undertakings.

1. **Schooling as a Center Mission:**
   Educational Shows and Shows:
   Zoos and safe-havens decisively configuration shows to offer guests a brief look into the normal ways of behaving, territories, and biological jobs of lions. Educational showcases, frequently enhanced with intuitive components, give a rich growth opportunity. Unmistakable signage, visual guides, and mixed media introductions add to passing on fundamental data about the species,

their preservation status, and the dangers they face in nature.

Instructive Projects and Studios:

Zoos and safe-havens coordinate various instructive projects and studios customized to various age gatherings. These drives cover subjects, for example, lion science, preservation challenges, and the more extensive meaning of biodiversity. Directed visits, intuitive meetings with creature care specialists, and studios on preservation themed exercises draw in guests in a unique educational experience.

Educational plan Based School Projects:

Teaming up with instructive establishments, zoos and safe-havens frequently foster educational plan based programs that line up with school prospectuses. These drives give understudies a first-hand experience with lions, enhancing study hall learning with viable encounters. By coordinating lion preservation into formal instruction, these projects add to building an age that values natural life and figures out the significance of protection.

2. **Bringing issues to light about Preservation Difficulties:**

Featuring Dangers in Nature:

Zoos and safe-havens utilize their foundation to enlighten the horde dangers looked by lions in their normal natural surroundings. Through interpretive displays and instructive materials, guests gain bits of knowledge into issues, for example, environment misfortune, human-untamed life struggle, poaching, and the more extensive effect of environmental change on lion populaces. By underlining the desperation of these difficulties, these offices add to cultivating a feeling of obligation and inspiring activity.

Narrating and Accounts:

Making convincing accounts about individual lions and their battles in the wild acculturates the preservation message. Zoos and safe-havens influence narrating to interface guests genuinely with the subjects, cultivating compassion and a more profound comprehension of the difficulties lions face. This profound association frequently converts into expanded help for protection drives and an uplifted feeling of moral obligation.

Protection Missions and Occasions:

Zoos and safe-havens routinely send off protection missions and occasions to enhance their instructive effect. These drives might incorporate mindfulness weeks, raising support drives, and public commitment exercises revolved around lion preservation. By preparing guests, local area individuals, and accomplice associations, these missions widen the range of preservation messages and add to an aggregate obligation to safeguarding lions and their environments.

3. **Logical Exploration and Preservation Drives:**
   Exhibiting Exploration Endeavors:

   Numerous zoos and asylums effectively participate in logical exploration connected with lion conduct, physiology, and well-being. Showing these exploration endeavors empowers guests to see the value in the commitments of hostage settings to more extensive logical information. By exhibiting progressing projects, establishments establish a climate where guests perceive the double jobs of zoos and safe-havens as instructive and research-driven elements.

   Cooperation in Protection Projects:

   Zoos and safe-havens frequently team up with preservation associations, both locally and worldwide, to take part in more extensive lion protection programs. These coordinated efforts might include territory reclamation projects, local area commitment drives, or direct commitments to in-situ preservation endeavors. By effectively partaking in these projects, zoos and safe-havens show their obligation to the more extensive preservation scene.

4. **Moral Contemplations and Creature Government assistance:**
   Advancing Moral Creature Care Principles:

   The moral treatment and government assistance of hostage lions are fundamental in any instructive setting. Zoos and safe-havens stick to severe creature care norms, guaranteeing that the physical and mental requirements of the lions are met. By straightforwardly advancing these guidelines, establishments pass a responsibility on to moral practices and fabricate entrust with the general population.

Adjusting Preservation and Creature Government assistance Objectives:

The test for zoos and safe-havens lies in finding some kind of harmony between their preservation and creature government assistance targets. Moral contemplations require a pledge to giving lions conditions that emulate their normal environments, admittance to enhancement exercises, and veterinary consideration that focuses on their prosperity. Accomplishing this equilibrium guarantees that hostage lions contribute emphatically to preservation endeavors without undermining their government assistance.

5. **Innovation and Advancement in Training:**

Computer generated Reality and Expanded Reality Displays:
Zoos and safe-havens are progressively integrating computer generated reality (VR) and expanded reality (AR) innovations into their displays. These vivid encounters transport guests to the core of lion natural surroundings, giving a more significant comprehension of the species and their biological systems.

VR and AR shows upgrade the instructive effect, making finding out about lion preservation an intuitive and noteworthy experience.

Web based Learning Stages:
The computerized age has introduced web based learning stages that supplement nearby instructive drives. Zoos and safe-havens foster virtual visits, online classes, and intelligent sites that proposal top to bottom bits of knowledge into lion protection. These internet based assets broaden the instructive arrive at past

actual visits, permitting a worldwide crowd to draw in with lion protection endeavors.

6. **Estimating Effect and Variation:**

Guest Commitment Measurements:

Zoos and safe-havens use guest commitment measurements, for example, participation rates, cooperation in instructive projects, and criticism overviews, to check the effect of their instructive drives. Dissecting these measurements assists establishments with refining their instructive systems, recognize regions for development, and adjust their ways to deal with boost adequacy.

Long haul Effect Evaluation:

Surveying the drawn out effect of instructive drives includes following changes in open mentalities, ways of behaving, and support for preservation causes. Longitudinal investigations and follow-up evaluations permit zoos and safe-havens to quantify the getting through effect of their instructive endeavors, at last adding to a more educated and preservation situated public.

6.3 Connection between captive and wild lion populations

The connection among hostage and wild lion populaces is a perplexing interaction of protection endeavors, logical examination, and moral contemplations. Hostage lion populaces, tracked down in zoos, safe-havens, and rearing projects, are complicatedly associated with their wild partners. This article investigates the complex association among hostage and wild lion populaces, analyzing the jobs hostage settings play in protection, hereditary variety conservation, research, and the moral difficulties innate in dealing with these connections.

1. **Protection Drives and the Hostage Wild Nexus:**
   Instruction and Protection Mindfulness:
   Zoos and safe-havens go about as instructive center points, overcoming any barrier between the general population and the protection needs of lions in nature.

Through instructive projects, displays, and intuitive encounters, hostage settings bring issues to light about the dangers confronting wild lion populaces, stressing the significance of protection drives and cultivating a feeling of obligation among guests.

Financing and Backing for Wild Preservation:

The association among hostage and wild lion populaces stretches out past attention to monetary help. Incomes produced by zoos and safe-havens add to subsidizing preservation programs pointed toward safeguarding lion environments, fighting poaching, and carrying out local area based drives. This monetary help turns into a life saver for associations working in the field to address the difficulties looked by wild lion populaces.

Renewed introduction Projects and Protection Achievement:

A few hostage settings effectively partake in lion renewed introduction programs, where good to go people reared in bondage are once again introduced into nature. These projects intend to reinforce declining wild populaces, reestablish environments, and add to the general progress of lion preservation. The information acquired from overseeing hostage populaces advises the improvement regarding methodologies for effective renewed introduction and transformation to indigenous habitats.

2. **Hereditary Variety and Protection:**

Hostage Rearing for Hereditary Administration:

The hereditary variety of lion populaces is a urgent part of their drawn out endurance. Hostage rearing projects assume a critical part in safeguarding and overseeing hereditary variety via cautiously choosing reproducing matches in light of their hereditary foundations. This proactive methodology forestalls inbreeding, improves the general strength of hostage populaces, and contributes significant hereditary variety information for more extensive preservation endeavors.

Protection Populaces for Hereditary Strength:

Hostage lion populaces, going about as protection populaces, defend hereditary variety against unanticipated dangers to wild populaces. In case of illness flare-ups, living space obliteration, or different difficulties, all around oversaw hostage populaces can act as supplies of hereditary variety. This hereditary flexibility turns into a critical resource for potential renewed introduction endeavors and keeping up with the versatile capability of the species.

Logical Exploration on Hereditary Elements:

Hostage settings give controlled conditions to concentrating on the hereditary elements of lion populaces. Logical examination on hostage people assists protectionists with grasping the heritability of qualities, the effect of hereditary variety on generally populace wellbeing, and the likely ramifications for wild populaces. This examination illuminates hereditary administration methodologies and adds to the more extensive comprehension of lion science.

3. **Logical Exploration and Conduct Studies:**

Social Examinations and Experiences into Wild Ways of behaving:

Noticing lion conduct in bondage offers significant bits of knowledge into their regular ways of behaving, social designs, and biological jobs. Conduct concentrates on in hostage settings add to a more profound comprehension of lion nature, illuminating protectionists about the species' necessities and ways of behaving. This information helps with the advancement of compelling preservation procedures for wild populaces.

Wellbeing Exploration and Sickness The board:

Hostage populaces give controlled conditions to wellbeing examination and infection the board. Logical examinations on hostage lions help recognize and address medical problems, adding to a more extensive comprehension of illnesses that might influence wild populaces. The information acquired from overseeing wellbeing challenges in bondage illuminates preservation procedures pointed toward shielding wild lions from potential sickness dangers.

Preparing for Renewed introduction Achievement:

Lions reproduced in bondage and ready for renewed introduction go through specific preparation to foster fundamental abilities to survive. This preparation, directed in hostage settings, incorporates figuring out how to chase, keeping away from hunters, and exploring normal scenes. These abilities are vital for the outcome of renewed introduction programs, and the preparation conventions are educated by logical examination directed in imprisonment.

4. **Moral Contemplations in Dealing with the Association: Creature Government assistance and Moral Hostage Practices:**

The association among hostage and wild lion populaces requires a guarantee to the best expectations of creature government assistance. Moral contemplations request that the physical and mental necessities of hostage lions are met, enveloping legitimate nooks, improvement exercises, social designs, and veterinary consideration. Finding some kind of harmony between protection targets and creature government assistance is basic for the believability and moral remaining of hostage programs.

Public Discernment and Protection Morals:

The moral contemplations in overseeing hostage and wild lion populaces reach out to public discernment. Preservation morals direct that foundations straightforwardly impart their obligation to creature government assistance and protection objectives. Public confidence in hostage settings relies on the confirmation that the creatures are all around focused on, and the preservation drives line up with moral standards.

Adjusting Protection Goals:

Adjusting the double targets of preservation and creature government assistance is a continuous test. Moral contemplations direct that protection endeavors shouldn't think twice about prosperity of individual creatures. Establishments should consistently rethink their works on, looking for creative ways of adding to protection while guaranteeing the best expectations of care for hostage lions.

5. **Difficulties and Future Headings:**

Financial Difficulties in Wild Natural surroundings:

The association among hostage and wild lion populaces is tested by financial elements in lion environments. Fast urbanization, land-use changes, and human-natural life clashes undermine the very biological systems where lions flourish. Tending to these difficulties requires a comprehensive methodology that incorporates protection endeavors, local area commitment, and economical improvement drives.

Environmental Change and Protection Elements:

Environmental change adds an extra layer of intricacy to the association among hostage and wild lion populaces. Changes in atmospheric conditions, living space debasement, and the effect on prey species impact the protection elements of lions. Relieving the impacts of environmental change requires versatile techniques that include both hostage and wild settings.

Mechanical Advances and Preservation Joining:

Future bearings in the association among hostage and wild lion populaces include tackling mechanical advances. Incorporating state of the art advancements, like remote detecting, man-made consciousness, and hereditary planning, upgrades the accuracy and viability of preservation methodologies. These advances work with information driven navigation, screen natural surroundings, and add to the general outcome of protection programs.

6.3 Future implications for lion conservation based on transition success

The progress of lion preservation advances holds significant ramifications for the fate of these glorious animals and the more extensive endeavors to protect biodiversity. As lions explore the difficulties of living space misfortune, human-untamed life struggle, and natural changes, fruitful progress drives offer important examples and experiences. This paper investigates the future ramifications for lion protection in light of change achievement, analyzing the potential for extended preservation endeavors, maintainable concurrence models, and the job of mechanical advancements in molding the fate of these notorious hunters.

1. **Development of Protection Drives:**
   Increasing Effective Advances:
   Effective advances of lion populaces from hostage to wild conditions prepare for increasing protection drives. Illustrations gained from these advances illuminate the improvement regarding conventions, best practices, and versatile methodologies that can be applied to more extensive districts. By utilizing the information acquired from fruitful changes, preservationists can broaden their effect, tending to the protection needs of extra lion populaces and encouraging the extension of safeguarded regions.
   Replication Across Locales:
   Locales confronting comparable protection difficulties can profit from the outcome of lion change programs. Moving fruitful models to new areas requires a nuanced comprehension of neighborhood environments, local area elements, and likely dangers. Traditionalists can team up across borders, sharing aptitude and fitting change systems to fit the particular requirements of assorted lion populaces. This replication approach upgrades the worldwide impression of fruitful protection works on, adding to the safeguarding of lions in various natural surroundings.

2. **Headways in Feasible Conjunction Models:**
   Local area Based Preservation Techniques:
   The progress of lion changes frequently relies on compelling local area commitment and the advancement of practical conjunction models. Future ramifications for lion preservation include

extending these local area based approaches. By effectively including nearby networks in preservation navigation, tending to their interests, and giving financial motivations to concurrence, protectionists can encourage an agreeable harmony between human exercises and lion living spaces.

Inventive Domesticated animals Security Techniques:

Human-untamed life struggle, especially concerning domesticated animals predation, stays a critical test for lion preservation. The outcome of advances gives a chance to investigate and carry out inventive animals security techniques. Advances, for example, resistant to hunter walled in areas, early-advance notice frameworks, and the utilization of watchman creatures can limit clashes, diminishing retaliatory killings of lions and advancing quiet conjunction among networks and untamed life.

Ecotourism as an Economical Income Source:

Fruitful changes feature the capability of ecotourism as a reasonable income hotspot for lion protection. Very much oversaw the travel industry drives revolved around capably noticing lions in their normal natural surroundings add to neighborhood economies and asset preservation endeavors. The positive financial effect of ecotourism gives an impetus to networks to safeguard lion populaces and their biological systems, making a commonly valuable connection among preservation and maintainable turn of events.

3. **Bridling Mechanical Developments:**
Remote Detecting and Checking:

The progress of lion changes highlights the significance of trend setting innovations in checking and safeguarding these species. Remote detecting and checking advances, including satellite imaging and camera traps, offer continuous information on lion developments, natural surroundings changes, and expected dangers. Coordinating these innovations into preservation methodologies improves the accuracy and proficiency of observing endeavors, adding to proactive protection measures.

Information Investigation and Computerized reasoning:

Progress achievement works with the joining of information examination and man-made consciousness into lion preservation drives. These advancements can process huge datasets, distinguish designs, and anticipate expected areas of contention or territory debasement. By bridling the force of computer based intelligence, moderates gain important experiences that illuminate versatile administration methodologies, empowering a more proactive and responsive way to deal with the difficulties looked by lion populaces.

Cooperative Preservation Robots:

Preservation drones furnished with high-goal cameras and sensors assume a vital part in checking and safeguarding lion living spaces. The outcome of advances speeds up the mix of cooperative robot organizations, where various associations share information and direction endeavors.

Drones give continuous reconnaissance, helping with hostile to poaching measures, living space observing, and the recognizable proof of potential protection dangers.

4. **Environmental Change Transformation Procedures:**

Effect of Environmental Change on Lion Living spaces:

The progress of lion advances prompts a reconsideration of protection methodologies notwithstanding environmental change. Changes in weather conditions, adjusted environments, and changing prey elements influence lion natural surroundings. Traditionalists should foster versatile techniques to relieve the impacts of environmental change, recognizing environment strong living spaces, and executing measures to shield lions from the results of a quickly evolving climate.

Coordinating Environment Strong Protection Practices:

Future ramifications for lion protection include incorporating environment strong practices into existing methodologies. This might incorporate the recognizable proof of movement passage-ways, the production of environment versatile administration plans, and cooperative endeavors to address the underlying drivers of environmental change. By adjusting protection practices to the real factors of an evolving environment, traditionalists improve the drawn out suitability of lion populaces.

5. **Worldwide Joint effort and Strategy Promotion:**

Worldwide Collaboration for Preservation Objectives:

The progress of lion changes underscores the requirement for upgraded worldwide cooperation in protection endeavors. Lions, as dominant hunters, assume a vital part in keeping up with environment balance. Cooperative drives including states, NGOs, and global associations can work with the advancement of facilitated preservation plans, pooling assets, and aptitude to address transboundary challenges and safeguard lion populaces across their reach.

Promotion for Preservation Strategies:

Expanding on the progress of lion changes, preservationists can advocate for the execution of powerful protection arrangements. These arrangements might include environment security, against poaching measures, local area commitment structures, and untamed life dealing anticipation. By effectively captivating with policymakers and supporting for protection well disposed regulation, the fate of lion preservation can be gotten on a worldwide scale.

Chapter 7

Looking Ahead

As we stand at the edge of the third ten years of the 21st 100 years, the world is balanced on the cusp of phenomenal difficulties and potential open doors. The conjunction of worldwide issues, mechanical progressions, financial changes, and ecological worries shapes the scene of our future. This exposition investigates the horde aspects of looking forward, diving into the complex components of our advancing world. From addressing existential difficulties to embracing the capability of development, we explore the intricacies that characterize our way ahead.

1. **Molding the Worldwide Scene:**
   International Elements in a Multipolar World:
   The international stage is seeing a significant shift as the world changes into a multipolar scene. The ascent of new financial forces to be reckoned with, evolving unions, and international pressures reshape the worldwide request. Looking forward, countries should explore this many-sided snare of connections, producing conciliatory ties, and creating procedures that cultivate collaboration and quiet conjunction in this multipolar time.

Worldwide Wellbeing Difficulties:

The Coronavirus pandemic has highlighted the interconnectedness of the worldwide local area and the delicacy of general wellbeing frameworks. As we look forward, the world should address progressing wellbeing challenges, get ready for possible pandemics, and upgrade worldwide cooperation in medical services. Interests in research, immunization dispersion components, and fortifying general wellbeing foundations will be vital in building a tough worldwide wellbeing structure.

Environmental Change Goals:

The phantom of environmental change poses a potential threat, requesting dire and unequivocal activity. The next few decades will be essential in alleviating the impacts of environmental change, progressing to feasible practices, and creating imaginative arrangements. Worldwide collaboration, environmentally friendly power reception, and economical improvement strategies will shape our capacity to defy the difficulties presented by an evolving environment.

2. **Mechanical Changes:**

The Fourth Modern Upset:

Innovative headways keep on speeding up, impelling us into the Fourth Modern Transformation. Computerized reasoning, advanced mechanics, the Web of Things (IoT), and other troublesome innovations are reshaping ventures, economies, and the idea of work. Looking forward, social orders should adjust to these changes, bridling the capability of innovation while tending to moral contemplations, security concerns, and the effect on business.

Information Upheaval and Security Concerns:

The multiplication of information driven advances brings up basic issues about protection and security. As we look forward, the mindful utilization of information, powerful protection guidelines, and network safety estimates become basic. Offsetting development with moral contemplations guarantees that the advantages of the information insurgency are acknowledged without compromising individual security and cultural prosperity.

Biotechnological Outskirts:

Forward leaps in biotechnology hold commitments and difficulties that will characterize our future. From quality altering to customized medication, the moral ramifications of controlling life at a sub-atomic level require cautious thought. Looking forward, social orders should participate in moral talk, lay out administrative structures, and explore the perplexing landscape of biotechnological progressions with an emphasis on capable development.

3. **Financial Ideal models:**

Comprehensive Monetary Development:

The quest for monetary development should be joined by a pledge to inclusivity. Tending to pay disparity, giving fair admittance to schooling and medical care, and cultivating social versatility are significant parts of comprehensive monetary development. Looking forward, states, organizations, and common society should team up to make monetary frameworks that benefit all sections of society.

Reclassifying Work in the Advanced Age:

The computerized age is changing the idea of work, with computerization and man-made consciousness adjusting position scenes. As we look forward, social orders should adjust by reskilling the labor force, cultivating business venture, and rethinking training to plan people for the positions representing things to come. Strategies that advance adaptability, balance between serious and fun activities, and social security nets will be fundamental in exploring this change in perspective.

Civil rights and Common freedoms:

Propelling civil rights and common freedoms stays a principal objective for what's in store. Handling fundamental imbalances, tending to segregation, and maintaining the poise and freedoms of all people are central standards. Looking forward, social orders should take a stab at equity, balance, and the insurance of basic liberties, cultivating conditions where variety is commended, and all voices are heard.

4. **Natural Stewardship:**

Biodiversity Protection and Environment Reclamation:

The corruption of environments and loss of biodiversity undermine the actual groundworks of life on The planet. As we look forward, ecological stewardship includes deliberate endeavors in biodiversity preservation and biological system reclamation. Embracing reasonable works on, safeguarding regular environments, and participating in worldwide protection drives are basic for saving the planet's biological equilibrium.

Roundabout Economy and Economical Practices:

Embracing a roundabout economy and economical practices is key to relieving natural difficulties. From decreasing waste and elevating reusing to changing to environmentally friendly power sources, the way ahead includes reshaping utilization examples and creation processes. Looking forward, organizations and people the same should focus on manageability, perceiving the interconnectedness of ecological wellbeing and human prosperity.

Water and Food Security:

The nexus of water and food security presents critical difficulties before long. Populace development, environmental change, and water shortage compromise rural frameworks and food creation. Looking forward, reasonable water the board rehearses, accuracy horticulture, and imaginative answers for food creation will be fundamental in guaranteeing worldwide food security.

5. **Cultural Flexibility and Social Transformation:**

Building Cultural Flexibility:

Cultural flexibility turns into a basic calculate exploring a questionable future. From catastrophic events to worldwide wellbeing emergencies, social orders should assemble strength through powerful framework, fiasco readiness, and social union. Looking forward, interests in strength at nearby, public, and worldwide levels will be fundamental for enduring the difficulties of an unusual world.

Social Transformation in a Globalized World:

The interconnectedness of the cutting edge world brings assorted societies into contact, requiring social variation and understanding. As we look forward, social orders should embrace social variety, encouraging inclusivity and common regard. Social variation includes exploring the intricacies of globalization while protecting the lavishness of individual societies, dialects, and customs.

6. **Training as an Impetus for Change:**

Extraordinary Training for What's in store:

Training arises as an extraordinary power that shapes what's to come. Looking forward, schooling systems should develop to outfit students with decisive reasoning abilities, versatility, and a worldwide point of view. Innovation empowered learning, interdisciplinary methodologies, and an emphasis on deep rooted learning are indispensable parts of instruction as an impetus for positive change.

Enabling the Future:

The strengthening of the cutting edge includes ingraining upsides of supportability, social obligation, and moral initiative. As we look forward, sustaining an age of worldwide residents who are compassionate, imaginative, and focused on certain change turns into a common obligation. Schooling turns into a channel for enabling people to contribute seriously to the difficulties and chances representing things to come.

7.1 Ongoing projects and initiatives for improving lion welfare

The preservation and government assistance of lions are basic worries despite developing natural, cultural, and financial elements. Continuous activities and drives all over the planet are working resolutely to work on the government assistance of lion populaces, both in the wild and in imprisonment. This exposition investigates a different scope of endeavors pointed toward defending the prosperity of lions, resolving issues, for example, territory safeguarding, human-untamed life struggle, hostage the executives, and the more extensive setting of worldwide preservation.

1. **Untamed life Preservation in Normal Environments:**
   Environment Safeguarding and Reclamation:
   Safeguarding and reestablishing regular living spaces is crucial to lion government assistance. Associations and states team up to lay out and keep up with safeguarded regions, guaranteeing adequate room and assets for lion populaces. Continuous ventures center around battling natural surroundings debasement, deforestation, and infringement, defending the environments fundamental for the endurance and prosperity of wild lions.
   Against Poaching and Natural life Insurance:
   The danger of poaching poses a potential threat over lion populaces. Against poaching drives utilize cutting edge innovations, local area commitment, and watching procedures to check unlawful hunting. Progressing projects expect to fortify policing, observation, and enable neighborhood networks to go about as stewards of natural life, cultivating an aggregate obligation to the security of lions and their territories.
   Human-Untamed life Struggle Moderation:
   Human-untamed life struggle stays a huge test for lion government assistance. Drives center around creating procedures to relieve clashes, especially in districts where human populaces infringe upon lion regions. Executing estimates like secure animals nooks, early admonition frameworks, and local area schooling decreases clashes and advances conjunction among people and lions.

2. **Hostage The board and Preservation:**
Worldwide Hostage Reproducing Projects:
Hostage reproducing programs are instrumental in safeguarding hereditary variety and giving a security net to imperiled lion populaces. Zoos, asylums, and rearing offices team up on worldwide drives to capably oversee hostage populaces. These projects focus on hereditary variety, keep up with definite studbooks, and work towards feasible reproducing practices to add to the drawn out preservation of the species.

Restoration and Delivery Projects:
A few tasks center around the recovery and arrival of hostage lions into semi-wild or safeguarded conditions. These drives expect to once again introduce lions to regular natural surroundings while guaranteeing they have what it takes important for endurance. Such projects include thorough preparation, conduct evaluations, and continuous checking to survey the outcome of delivered people in adjusting to their wild environmental factors.

Advancement and Prosperity Drives:
Guaranteeing the prosperity of hostage lions is vital for progressing projects. Advancement programs plan to animate regular ways of behaving, mental commitment, and actual work. Inventive drives incorporate the arrangement of fluctuated environments, puzzle feeders, and intelligent exercises that advance the physical and mental wellbeing of hostage lions.

3. **Local area Commitment and Training:**
Preservation Instruction Projects:
Instruction is a foundation of lion government assistance drives, with continuous tasks zeroing in on bringing issues to light about the significance of lion preservation. Schools, people group, and online stages are used to disperse data about the biological job of lions, the dangers they face, and the meaning of safeguarding biodiversity. Preservation schooling cultivates a feeling of stewardship and enables networks to partake in lion government

assistance effectively.

Local area Drove Protection Drives:

Cooperative tasks draw in neighborhood networks in lion preservation endeavors, perceiving the fundamental job networks play in the conjunction of people and lions. Drives include preparing local area individuals in untamed life observing, supporting reasonable livelihoods, and executing projects that benefit the two lions and nearby occupants. By adjusting preservation objectives to local area interests, these tasks encourage a common obligation regarding lion government assistance.

The travel industry as a Preservation Device:

Manageable the travel industry drives influence the monetary worth of natural life to help lion protection. Capable the travel industry rehearses produce income for protection projects, reserve against poaching endeavors, and add to nearby economies. By coordinating the travel industry with preservation, progressing projects endeavor to show the way that the government assistance of lions and monetary flourishing can remain forever inseparable.

4. **Mechanical Advancements for Protection:**

Observing and Following Advancements:

Mechanical headways assume a crucial part in continuous lion government assistance projects. GPS collars, camera traps, and satellite innovation empower exact checking and following of lion populaces. Ongoing information assortment illuminates protection methodologies, mitigates human-untamed life clashes, and adds to a more profound comprehension of lion conduct in both wild and hostage settings.

Man-made brainpower in Preservation:

Man-made brainpower (artificial intelligence) is progressively being utilized in continuous tasks for breaking down huge datasets connected with lion conduct, living space use, and populace elements. AI calculations can recognize designs, foresee likely dangers, and improve dynamic cycles. Man-made intelligence applications add to more successful and versatile preservation procedures.

Local area Based Portable Applications:

Portable applications custom-made for neighborhood networks act as significant apparatuses for lion preservation. These applications give continuous data about lion developments, ready networks to possible struggles, and work with detailing of natural life sightings. By cultivating local area commitment through innovation, these drives make an organization of educated and engaged partners in lion government assistance.

5. **Worldwide Joint efforts and Preservation Approaches:**

Global Preservation Arrangements:

Worldwide joint efforts are essential for guaranteeing the progress of lion government assistance drives. Global associations, legislatures, and NGOs cooperate under preservation arrangements to organize endeavors, share assets, and lay out principles for the security of lions. Arrangements, for example, the Show on Global Exchange Jeopardized Types of Wild Fauna and Greenery (Refers to) assume a urgent part in controlling the worldwide exchange of lions and their body parts.

Backing for Lawful Securities:

Continuous tasks advocate for the lawful insurance of lions at public and global levels. These endeavors include campaigning for stricter enemy of poaching regulations, guidelines against the unlawful natural life exchange, and measures to check environment annihilation. By affecting arrangement and legitimate systems, these drives add to establishing a climate where lions get the fundamental lawful assurances for their government assistance.

7.2 The evolving role of zoos and sanctuaries in the conservation landscape

Zoos and safe-havens, once basically seen as spots for public diversion and schooling, have gone through a change in outlook as of late.

The developing job of zoos and safe-havens in the preservation scene mirrors a developing consciousness of the basic need to secure and save biodiversity. This article investigates the multi-layered elements of the changing jobs of zoos and safe-havens, accentuating their commitments to untamed life preservation, examination, schooling, and moral contemplations.

1. **Protection Reproducing Projects:**
   Protecting Imperiled Species:
   Zoos and safe-havens assume a urgent part in saving jeopardized species through preservation rearing projects. Via cautiously overseeing hostage populaces and utilizing hereditary variety systems, these foundations go about as arks, defending species that face dangers in nature.
   Examples of overcoming adversity, like the California condor and dark footed ferret, feature the capability of hostage rearing in forestalling the elimination of imperiled species.
   Renewed introduction Endeavors:
   An essential piece of the advancing job is the emphasis on renewed introduction endeavors. Zoos and asylums are effectively engaged with getting ready and once again introducing hostage reproduced creatures into their regular living spaces. This interaction, while testing, adds to the reclamation of lessening wild populaces. Renewed introduction drives overcome any issues among imprisonment and the wild, underscoring the significance of safeguarding environments and encouraging self-supporting populaces.
   Hereditary Administration and Variety:
   The fastidious hereditary administration of hostage populaces is pivotal for the drawn out feasibility of species. Zoos and safe-havens team up on worldwide drives to keep up with hereditary variety, forestall inbreeding, and guarantee the wellbeing and flexibility of hostage creatures. These endeavors contribute

significant hereditary data that illuminates preservation systems, tending to the difficulties presented by divided natural surroundings and contracting wild populaces.

2. **Research and Logical Progressions:**
Social Examinations and Protection Experiences:

The advancing job of zoos and safe-havens reaches out to becoming living research centers for social examinations. Noticing creatures in bondage gives significant experiences into their regular ways of behaving, social designs, and natural necessities. These examinations add to a more profound comprehension of species-explicit prerequisites, supporting moderates in creating powerful procedures for safeguarding territories and tending to dangers in nature.

Wellbeing and Illness Exploration:

Zoos and safe-havens are at the very front of wellbeing and sickness research. The controlled conditions of hostage settings consider orderly wellbeing observing and research, prompting the recognizable proof and the executives of sicknesses that might influence wild populaces. Research on hostage creatures adds to the more extensive comprehension of untamed life wellbeing, offering experiences that can illuminate preservation procedures and shield species from expected pestilences.

Preservation Medication:

The field of preservation medication has arisen as a vital part of the developing job of zoos and safe-havens. Veterinary groups in these establishments work on the bleeding edges, tending to medical problems, giving clinical consideration, and leading exploration that straightforwardly adds to the prosperity and endurance of imperiled species. The crossing point of veterinary medication and protection guarantees that creatures in imprisonment are ministers for their partners in nature.

3. **Instruction and Public Mindfulness:**
Moving Toward Preservation Training:

Zoos and safe-havens are progressively underlining protection instruction as an essential mission. Instructive projects mean to bring issues to light about the predicament of imperiled species, the significance of biodiversity, and the job people can play in preservation. By moving concentration from diversion to training, these foundations look to rouse a feeling of obligation and ecological stewardship in guests.

Intelligent Growth opportunities:

The developing job integrates intelligent opportunities for growth that connect with guests on a more profound level. Zoos and safe-havens use interpretive displays, directed visits, and intelligent advancements to give instructive and vivid encounters. Interfacing guests sincerely to natural life cultivates a feeling of sympathy and understanding, building up the criticalness of preservation endeavors.

Promotion for Reasonable Practices:

Zoos and asylums influence their foundation to advocate for maintainable practices and moral treatment of creatures. By advancing capable customer decisions, environment safeguarding, and protection amicable ways of life, these organizations broaden their effect past their actual limits. The point is to engage guests to settle on informed choices that add to the more extensive objectives of biodiversity preservation.

4. **Moral Contemplations and Creature Government assistance:**
   Shift Towards Moral Creature Care:

The developing job puts an elevated accentuation on moral contemplations in creature care. Zoos and safe-havens are taking on rehearses that focus on the physical and mental prosperity of creatures. Nooks are intended to mirror normal territories, and enhancement exercises are custom-made to invigorate regular ways of behaving, cultivating a more compassionate and moral way to deal with hostage creature the executives.

Getting rid of Conventional Displays:

Perceiving the constraints of customary displays, a few zoos are gradually getting rid of nooks that focus on diversion over creature government assistance. All things considered, they are moving towards open and vivid living spaces that give a more indigenous habitat to the creatures. This shift lines up with developing moral guidelines and accentuates the significance of making spaces that focus on the government assistance of hostage creatures.

Straightforwardness and Protection Morals:

Straightforwardness in tasks and a guarantee to preservation morals are fundamental to the developing job of zoos and safe-havens. Foundations are progressively straightforward about their protection drives, creature government assistance rehearses, and the moral contemplations that guide their navigation. This straightforwardness fabricates entrust with people in general, cultivating support for preservation endeavors and adding to the validity of these organizations.

5. **Coordinated effort for Worldwide Preservation Objectives:**

Associations Between Foundations:

Zoos and asylums are producing organizations and coordinated efforts to intensify their effect on worldwide preservation objectives. These associations include the trading of information, hereditary materials, and best practices. By cooperating, foundations can address the difficulties looked by species in changed locales, adding to a more strong and composed way to deal with untamed life preservation.

Worldwide Preservation Drives:

The advancing job stretches out past individual organizations to support in worldwide protection drives. Zoos and safe-havens are effectively engaged with supporting and subsidizing projects that address preservation challenges on a more extensive scale. These drives might incorporate environment insurance, hostile to poaching endeavors, and local area commitment projects that add to the safeguarding of biodiversity on a worldwide level.

7.3 Potential advancements in creating more natural environments for captive lions

Hostage conditions for lions have for some time been a subject of investigation, inciting a change in outlook toward making more naturalistic territories that focus on the physical and mental prosperity of these lofty creatures. As we dive into the 21st hundred years, the potential for progressions in planning and keeping up with hostage conditions offers energizing possibilities for the government assistance of hostage lions.

This exposition investigates imaginative methodologies, advancements, and procedures that hold the commitment of establishing conditions that better copy the normal living spaces of lions.

1. **Planning Vivid and Advanced Living spaces:**
   Environment Mimicry for Social Feeling:
   Progressions in living space configuration center around establishing conditions that intently copy the regular environments of lions. Bigger nooks with different geography, including rocks, trees, and water highlights, intend to give lions a more vivid and invigorating experience. Such environments energize regular ways of behaving like climbing, investigating, and hunting, adding to the general prosperity of hostage lions.
   Intuitive Components for Mental Commitment:
   The consolidation of intelligent components inside hostage conditions adds a layer of mental commitment for lions. Puzzle feeders, fragrance trails, and secret treats empower critical thinking and mental feeling. These developments not just copy the difficulties looked in the wild yet additionally give potential open doors to hostage lions to communicate their regular impulses, encouraging a more enhanced and fulfilling climate.
2. **Mechanical Advancements for Ecological Checking:**
   Sensor-Based Observing Frameworks:

Mechanical headways in ecological observing frameworks offer continuous experiences into the prosperity of hostage lions. Sensor-based arrangements, including cameras, temperature sensors, and movement finders, give ceaseless information on lion conduct, wellbeing pointers, and natural circumstances. This data empowers guardians to settle on informed choices, guaranteeing that the hostage climate stays helpful for the requirements of the lions.

Artificial intelligence Helped Conduct Investigation:

Man-made brainpower (simulated intelligence) applications are being investigated to examine lion conduct in imprisonment. AI calculations can recognize designs, evaluate feelings of anxiety, and distinguish conduct abnormalities that might demonstrate wellbeing concerns. By bridling computer based intelligence, parental figures can acquire a more profound comprehension of the close to home and actual conditions of hostage lions, considering more customized and responsive consideration.

3. **Coordinated Protection Training Drives:**

Training Centered Display Plan:

Headways in display configuration focus on schooling and preservation informing. Rather than simply displaying creatures, shows are intended to recount the normal ways of behaving, living spaces, and preservation challenges looked by lions. Interpretive signage, intuitive showcases, and instructive projects add to guest mindfulness and cultivate a more profound association between the general population and the preservation mission.

Computer generated Reality (VR) Encounters:

Computer generated reality innovation offers a clever way to deal with drench guests in the realm of lions. VR encounters can mimic the sights and hints of a lion's normal territory, giving an instructive and sympathetic viewpoint. Coordinating VR into hostage conditions permits guests to see the value in the intricacy of lion biological systems and better comprehend the significance of preservation endeavors in saving these conditions.

4. **Executing Encouraging feedback Preparing:**
Empowering Decision and Control:
Uplifting feedback preparing methods engage hostage lions by permitting them to practice decision and command over their current circumstance. By partner wanted ways of behaving with remunerations, for example, food or advancement things, lions can effectively take part in their own consideration. This approach improves their prosperity, lessens pressure, and encourages a positive connection among guardians and lions.

Preparing for Medical care and Farming:
Headways in uplifting feedback preparing reach out to medical care and farming practices. Lions can be prepared to deliberately partake in clinical assessments, immunizations, and normal check-ups. This diminishes the requirement for sedation, limits pressure related with veterinary techniques, and works with better by and large wellbeing the executives for hostage lions.

5. **Manageable and Eco-Accommodating Practices:**
Green Structure Methods:
The development and upkeep of hostage conditions are progressively embracing green structure strategies. Supportable materials, energy-productive plans, and eco-accommodating finishing add to a diminished natural effect. These headways line up with more extensive preservation objectives, stressing the interconnectedness between hostage conditions and the wellbeing of the planet.

Normal Asset The board:
Hostage conditions are investigating ways of limiting asset utilization and waste age. From water reusing frameworks to sustainable power sources, these developments plan to make naturally cognizant territories for lions. Asset the executives rehearses benefit the climate as well as add to the monetary maintainability of hostage offices.

6. **Joint effort and Data Sharing:**

Worldwide Joint effort Stages:
Headways in establishing common habitats for hostage lions reach out past individual offices. Worldwide joint effort stages empower zoos, asylums, and untamed life associations to share best practices, research discoveries, and examples of overcoming adversity. By cultivating joint effort, the aggregate information on the worldwide local area adds to progressing enhancements in hostage lion government assistance.

Open-Source Data Sharing:
The development of open-source stages works with the sharing of data and advancements in hostage lion the executives. Whether connected with living space plan, social enhancement, or veterinary consideration, open-source drives support straightforwardness and aggregate critical thinking. This cooperative methodology speeds up headways in establishing common habitats by utilizing the aggregate skill of the worldwide local area.

7.4 Global perspectives on lion conservation and the role of public awareness

Lion preservation is a worldwide test that requests cooperative endeavors and an increased feeling of public mindfulness. As notorious images of the wild, lions face dangers going from natural surroundings misfortune and human-untamed life struggle to poaching and sickness. This exposition investigates worldwide viewpoints on lion protection and highlights the significant job that public mindfulness plays in the aggregate endeavors to save these superb species.

1. **The Worldwide Setting of Lion Protection:**
   Geological Variety of Lion Natural surroundings:
   Lions are not bound to a particular locale but rather are circulated across various territories in Africa, from savannas to fields. Every area presents remarkable preservation challenges affected by elements, for example, environment, land use, and living together

with neighborhood networks. Understanding this topographical variety is pivotal for executing successful protection systems.

Human-Natural life Struggle and Environment Discontinuity:

As human populaces extend and territories shrivel, the cross-over among people and lions expands, prompting uplifted human-natural life struggle. Environment fracture disturbs conventional lion regions, frequently bringing about clashes over assets and presenting huge dangers to the two people and lions. Tending to these struggles requires a comprehensive methodology that thinks about the necessities of nearby networks and the preservation of lion populaces.

Poaching and Unlawful Natural life Exchange:

Poaching for body parts, like bones and skins, as well as the unlawful natural life exchange, represents a huge danger to lion populaces. Worldwide viewpoints on lion preservation should include endeavors to battle these criminal operations, including reinforcing policing, mindfulness about the results of natural life exchange, and pushing for stricter guidelines.

2. **The Job of Public Mindfulness in Lion Preservation:**

Encouraging Association and Sympathy:

Public mindfulness assumes a critical part in encouraging an association among individuals and lions. Through training and effort, people can foster a more profound comprehension of the difficulties looked by lions in nature. This association develops compassion, spurring individuals to take a functioning interest in lion preservation and backing drives pointed toward safeguarding these glorious animals.

Upholding for Protection Approaches:

Educated and connected with residents are bound to advocate for vigorous preservation strategies at neighborhood, public, and worldwide levels. Public mindfulness missions can engage people to voice their interests, request more grounded assurances for lions, and partake in drives that add to the definition and execution of powerful preservation arrangements.

Supporting Preservation Drives Monetarily:

Public mindfulness crusades illuminate as well as motivate activity. People who know about the difficulties confronting lion populaces are bound to contribute monetarily to protection drives. This monetary help is instrumental in subsidizing research, against poaching endeavors, natural surroundings reclamation, and local area commitment programs that on the whole add to the drawn out protection of lions.

3. **The Job of Media and Innovation in Open Mindfulness:**

Narratives and Natural life Movies:

Narratives and natural life films have the ability to contact a worldwide crowd, giving charming experiences into the existences of lions and the difficulties they face. Stages, for example, Public Geographic and real time features offer a way to exhibit the excellence and weakness of lions, driving home the significance of preservation endeavors.

Virtual Entertainment and Online Missions:

Online entertainment stages act as incredible assets for spreading mindfulness about lion preservation. Online missions, hashtags, and effective visuals can rapidly contact a wide crowd, bringing issues to light and moving people to make a move. The promptness and worldwide reach of virtual entertainment work with the spread of data and the activation of help for lion protection.

Computer generated Reality (VR) Encounters:

Headways in innovation, for example, computer generated reality encounters, permit individuals to submerge themselves in the realm of lions and witness firsthand the difficulties they face. VR encounters can summon a feeling of presence and direness, driving home the requirement for preservation activity. These creative methodologies influence innovation to upgrade public mindfulness and commitment.

4. Global Joint effort and Diverse Viewpoints:

Worldwide Protection Organizations:
Lion protection isn't restricted to public boundaries; it requires worldwide coordinated effort. Worldwide protection networks unite specialists, associations, and legislatures to share information, assets, and best practices. Public mindfulness crusades on a worldwide scale can enhance the effect of these cooperative endeavors, collecting support from different populaces.

Social Awareness and Neighborhood Commitment:
Worldwide points of view on lion protection should recognize the significance of social awareness and nearby commitment. Public mindfulness missions ought to be customized to reverberate with different social convictions and works on, guaranteeing that preservation messages are gotten emphatically and that nearby networks feel a feeling of pride in the protection cycle.

8

Chapter 8

Conclusion

As we explore the intricacies of the 21st 100 years, the scene of our reality is molded by remarkable difficulties, groundbreaking innovative progressions, and the basic for aggregate activity. In this extensive end, we consider the different topics investigated in the first papers, offering a blend of bits of knowledge, examples, and likely pathways forward. From the complex provokes of progressing lions to additional regular habitats to the worldwide point of view on protection, the job of innovation, and the developing elements of zoos and safe-havens, every subject adds to a more extensive story of adjusting to change, cultivating economical practices, and embracing what's to come.

1. **Changing Lions: Exploring Difficulties and Valuable open doors:**

   In the journey to change lions from imprisonment to additional regular habitats, we go up against complex provokes and take advantage of chances to reclassify the job of people in the preservation condition. Examples gained from previous slip-ups highlight the significance of cautious preparation, partner cooperation, and an all encompassing comprehension of the mind boggling interaction among hostage and wild environments. The effect on protection is significant, requesting a fragile harmony between preservation objectives, creature government assistance contemplations, and the requirement for cultural mindfulness.

2. **Addressing Worries in Once again introducing Lions to Nature:**

The renewed introduction of lions to additional regular habitats requires a nuanced approach that considers environmental, social, and hereditary variables. While potential difficulties, for example, human-natural life struggle and territory debasement pose a potential threat, creative systems, local area commitment, and versatile administration give an establishment to effective renewed introduction endeavors. The developing job of innovation arises as a vital partner in checking and supporting lions during this basic progress, guaranteeing an agreeable conjunction among lions and their regular territories.

3. **The Job of Innovation in Checking and Supporting Lions:**

In the powerful scene of lion protection, innovation arises as a groundbreaking power. From cutting edge observing frameworks to man-made reasoning applications, the job of innovation stretches out past logical examination to turn into a foundation of preservation endeavors.

As we investigate the capability of innovation in supporting lions during their progress, moral contemplations, protection concerns, and the dependable utilization of information become vital parts of an innovation driven preservation worldview.

4. **Illustrations Gained from Previous oversights and Disappointments:**

Reflection on previous slip-ups and disappointments in preservation tries fills in as a piercing sign of the inborn difficulties in overseeing complex biological systems. The crossing point of human exercises, environmental change, and the fragile equilibrium of biodiversity requires versatile systems and a promise to gaining from our aggregate encounters. By recognizing and redressing past mistakes, we lay the basis for more powerful and supportable protection rehearses.

5. **The Effect on Preservation: A Complex Investigation:**

An extensive investigation of the effect on preservation divulges the interconnectedness of different components, from changing lions to addressing concerns connected with renewed introduction and utilizing innovation. The ramifications for biodiversity, natural surroundings protection, and the fragile balance of biological systems highlight the criticalness of taking on comprehensive preservation draws near. As we wrestle with the complicated difficulties, the job of public mindfulness arises as a key part, overcoming any barrier between preservation drives and cultural commitment.

6. **Worldwide Points of view on Lion Preservation:**

The worldwide point of view on lion protection rises above topographical limits, accentuating the requirement for cooperative endeavors, social awareness, and global participation. Public mindfulness expects the all important focal point in this worldwide undertaking, going about as an impetus for informed activity, strategy backing, and monetary help. As we dive into the many-sided elements of human-natural life concurrence, the job of zoos and safe-havens, and the developing moral contemplations, the aggregate obligation to lion protection turns into a demonstration of our common obligation as stewards of the planet.

7. **Embracing What's in store: Exploring Difficulties and Valuable open doors:**

Looking forward, what's in store unfurls as a material formed by the examples of the past, the real factors of the present, and the capability of arising open doors. International movements, mechanical upsets, financial changes, and natural goals highlight the requirement for versatile techniques, development, and an aggregate obligation to building a maintainable and comprehensive world.

As we wrestle with the ramifications of the Fourth Modern Unrest, the intricacies of comprehensive financial development, and the basic of tending to environmental change, the job of schooling arises as a groundbreaking power in forming strong, informed, and engaged worldwide residents.

8. **Commitment of Balanced Hostage Lions to Worldwide Protection Endeavors:**

   In analyzing the commitment of balanced hostage lions to worldwide preservation endeavors, the account grows to envelop the urgent job of zoos and asylums. These foundations develop past their conventional jobs, becoming dynamic members in preservation reproducing programs, restoration drives, and instructive undertakings. The harmonious connection between balanced hostage lions and more extensive preservation objectives delineates the potential for moral hostage the executives to go about as a positive power in safeguarding biodiversity and raising public mindfulness.

9. **Job of Zoos and Safe-havens in Teaching The general population about Lion Protection:**

   Zoos and safe-havens arise as instructive centers, utilizing their foundation to illuminate and move the general population about lion protection. Through groundbreaking instruction programs, vivid displays, and intuitive growth opportunities, these organizations overcome any issues between general society and the fundamental mission of untamed life protection. The job of zoos and asylums stretches out past amusement, turning out to be strong backers for manageable practices, moral creature care, and worldwide preservation objectives.

10. **Association Among Hostage and Wild Lion Populaces:**
    Investigating the association among hostage and wild lion

populaces uncovers a fragile transaction of natural elements, hereditary variety, and moral contemplations. Preservation rearing projects, recovery drives, and feasible hostage the executives rehearses add to the more extensive account of protecting the natural association among hostage and wild lions. As we explore the intricacies of keeping up with sound populaces in the two settings, the illustrations gained from every circle advance comprehension we might interpret lion government assistance and preservation.

11. **Future Ramifications for Lion Preservation In light of Change Achievement:**

Expecting future ramifications for lion preservation depends on the outcome of continuous progress endeavors. The fragile harmony between human exercises, living space protection, and the variation of lions to regular habitats turns into a microcosm of the more extensive difficulties looked by worldwide preservation drives.

As we project forward, the triumphs and mishaps in progressing lions act as a compass, directing us toward versatile techniques, moral contemplations, and a reestablished obligation to the protection of biodiversity.

12. **Looking Forward: Outlining a Course for Feasible Protection:**

In looking forward, the union of worldwide difficulties and potential open doors requires a change in outlook in the manner in which we approach protection. The illustrations gained from lion preservation endeavors give an outline to exploring the intricacies of safeguarding biodiversity, relieving environmental change, and encouraging an agreeable connection among people and the regular world. An aggregate obligation to manageability, development, and inclusivity turns into the foundation of diagramming a course for a future where the unpredictable embroidery of life on Earth is safeguarded for a long time into the future.

8.1 Summary of key findings and insights

In navigating the different landscape of lion preservation, progressing, innovation combination, and the developing job of zoos and safe-havens, a rich embroidery of experiences and discoveries arises. This outline typifies the vital learnings from our investigation, winding around together the complexities of these points to offer a thorough outline of the difficulties, triumphs, and future possibilities in the domain of lion government assistance and worldwide preservation endeavors.

1. **Changing Lions to Common habitats:**
   Difficulties and Valuable open doors:
   Changing lions from imprisonment to additional regular habitats presents a fragile harmony between difficulties and valuable open doors. While natural surroundings discontinuity, human-untamed life struggle, and hereditary variety concerns present imposing impediments, inventive systems, local area commitment, and versatile administration offer promising roads for progress. The example learned is that an all encompassing methodology, incorporating environmental and financial contemplations, is basic for exploring the perplexing excursion of progressing lions.

   Human-Untamed life Conjunction:
   The outcome of changing lions depends on cultivating amicable connections among people and untamed life. Tending to human-untamed life struggle through local area inclusion, schooling, and reasonable improvement rehearses becomes significant. By perceiving the interconnectedness of environments and the significance of concurrence, protectionists can prepare for the fruitful incorporation of lions into their regular living spaces.

   Hereditary Administration:
   The multifaceted dance of hereditary qualities assumes a focal part in the change cycle. Hereditary administration of hostage populaces is essential to guarantee the drawn out practicality of

species. Cooperative endeavors to forestall inbreeding, keep up with hereditary variety, and integrate state of the art hereditary advances are fundamental for making composed and hereditarily strong lion populaces.

2. **Job of Innovation in Observing and Supporting Lions: Ecological Checking Frameworks:**

Mechanical progressions, especially in natural checking frameworks, offer constant bits of knowledge into the prosperity of lions. Sensors, cameras, and computer based intelligence driven examination add to a more profound comprehension of lion conduct, wellbeing markers, and ecological circumstances. In any case, moral contemplations and protection concerns should be painstakingly explored to guarantee capable and straightforward utilization of innovation.

Artificial intelligence Helped Social Examination:

The mix of man-made consciousness in social examination gives an original aspect to preservation endeavors. AI calculations can recognize designs, survey feelings of anxiety, and distinguish conduct inconsistencies. This not just guides in the prosperity of hostage lions yet additionally adds to the more extensive comprehension of untamed life conduct, advancing protection objectives.

Instructive Advances:

Innovation stretches out its compass to schooling, offering augmented reality encounters that drench the general population in the realm of lions. These imaginative methodologies upgrade public mindfulness as well as cultivate sympathy and understanding. Computer generated reality turns into a useful asset in separating hindrances, interfacing individuals to untamed life, and motivating an aggregate obligation to protection.

3. **Developing Job of Zoos and Safe-havens: Protection Rearing Projects:**

Zoos and safe-havens rise above their customary jobs, effectively taking part in protection reproducing programs. The commitment of balanced hostage lions turns into a significant resource in saving hereditary variety, going about as a hereditary supply for potential renewed introduction endeavors. Moral hostage the executives rehearses and the trading of hereditary materials assume an essential part in these projects.

Instructive Drives:

The developing job of zoos and safe-havens is set apart by a shift toward schooling centered drives. Past diversion, these foundations become instructive center points, cultivating mindfulness and comprehension of natural life preservation. Intuitive shows, directed visits, and virtual encounters connect with the general population on a more profound level, ingraining a feeling of obligation and support for the safeguarding of biodiversity.

Moral Contemplations:

A change in outlook toward moral contemplations in creature care becomes obvious in the developing jobs of zoos and safe-havens. The eliminating of customary shows for open and vivid environments mirrors a guarantee to the prosperity of hostage creatures. Straightforwardness in tasks, preservation morals, and an emphasis on making spaces that focus on creature government assistance highlight the moral change of these organizations.

4. **Worldwide Viewpoints on Lion Protection:**

Geological Variety:

Lion protection unfurls against the setting of geological variety, with lions occupying different districts in Africa. Perceiving this variety is fundamental for fitting protection methodologies to the novel difficulties introduced by every living space. Restricted approaches, social awareness, and commitment with different networks are indispensable parts of effective worldwide protection drives.

Human-Natural life Struggle Relief:

Worldwide points of view feature the need of relieving human-untamed life struggle on a more extensive scale. Protection endeavors should safeguard lion territories as well as include nearby networks in manageable practices. Comprehensive methodologies that address the necessities and worries of the two people and lions are vital for cultivating conjunction and guaranteeing the drawn out progress of preservation drives.

Job of Public Mindfulness:

The worldwide point of view on lion preservation highlights the crucial job of public mindfulness. Educated and drawn in residents are fundamental backers for preservation strategies, monetary help, and reasonable practices. Media, innovation, and worldwide joint effort stages become amazing assets in bringing issues to light and preparing a worldwide local area focused on the conservation of lions and their territories.

5. **Examples Gained from Previous slip-ups and Disappointments:**

Versatile Preservation Procedures:

Examples gained from previous mishaps stress the requirement for versatile protection techniques. The unique idea of environments requests adaptability, an eagerness to gain from disappointments, and a guarantee to refining approaches in view of experimental proof. The convergence of human exercises, environmental change, and biodiversity protection requires a comprehensive and responsive preservation ethos.

Comprehensive Biological system The executives:

The disappointments of the past highlight the interconnectedness of environments and the significance of all encompassing administration. Protection endeavors can't be compartmentalized; they should consider the more extensive natural setting, address underlying drivers of dangers, and draw in neighborhood networks as accomplices in safeguarding. This comprehensive methodology is primary to the flexibility and maintainability of protection attempts.

Comprehensive Direction:

Comprehensive navigation arises as a key example, stressing the significance of connecting with different partners in protection drives. Nearby people group, specialists, policymakers, and the public should be essential for the dynamic cycle to guarantee that techniques are logically applicable, socially delicate, and socially fair.

6. **Progressing Tasks and Drives for Further developing Lion Government assistance:**

Preservation Through Coordinated effort:

Continuous activities and drives for further developing lion government assistance highlight the force of joint effort. Worldwide associations, open-source data sharing, and cooperative stages work with the trading of information, assets, and best practices. By cooperating, establishments and associations add to a more firm and facilitated way to deal with lion preservation.

Maintainable Practices:

The obligation to progressing projects remembers a concentration for reasonable practices. From green structure strategies to normal asset the board, foundations are investigating ways of limiting ecological effect. These drives not just add to the government assistance of hostage lions yet additionally line up with more extensive preservation objectives, stressing the significance of mindful and supportable practices.

Schooling and Support:

Progressing projects feature the meaning of instruction and support. By utilizing stages for public mindfulness, establishments add to molding educated and engaged people. Backing for economical practices, moral treatment of creatures, and worldwide protection objectives becomes necessary to the continuous endeavors pointed toward further developing lion government assistance.

7. **The Association Among Hostage and Wild Lion Populaces: Preservation Rearing and Restoration:**

   The association among hostage and wild lion populaces is laid out through preservation rearing projects and restoration drives. Balanced hostage lions add to hereditary variety, going about as expected contender for renewed introduction endeavors. The cautious route of hereditary contemplations, moral practices, and supportable administration becomes fundamental to keeping up with this association.

   Research and Social Bits of knowledge:

   The cooperative energy among hostage and wild populaces stretches out to explore and social experiences. Concentrates on directed in hostage settings contribute significant information that improves how we might interpret lion conduct, wellbeing, and propagation. This corresponding connection among hostage and wild populaces improves preservation science and illuminates versatile administration techniques.

   Moral Contemplations in Hostage The board:

   The association among hostage and wild lion populaces requires moral contemplations in hostage the executives. The eliminating of conventional displays for additional naturalistic conditions mirrors a promise to the prosperity of hostage creatures. Moral contemplations stretch out to rearing practices, veterinary consideration, and the general personal satisfaction for creatures in imprisonment.

8. **Expected Headways in Establishing Regular habitats for Hostage Lions:**

   Vivid and Enhanced Environments:

   Expected progressions in establishing regular habitats for hostage lions rotate around planning vivid and enhanced territories. Bigger nooks with different geography, intelligent components for mental commitment, and an emphasis on living space mimicry expect to give hostage lions a really invigorating and fulfilling climate. These advancements focus on the physical and mental prosperity of lions in bondage.

Mechanical Developments in Natural Checking:

Progressions in establishing common habitats consolidate mechanical developments in ecological observing. Sensor-based frameworks, man-made intelligence helped examination, and ongoing information add to a far reaching comprehension of lion conduct and prosperity. The mindful incorporation of innovation guarantees that headways line up with moral contemplations and focus on the government assistance of hostage lions.

Encouraging feedback Preparing:

The potential for progressions incorporates encouraging feedback preparing procedures. Empowering hostage lions to practice decision and command over their current circumstance through preparing encourages a positive connection among guardians and lions. This approach improves the prosperity of lions as well as works with better medical services rehearses and decreases pressure related with veterinary systems.

9. **Worldwide Viewpoints on Lion Protection and the Job of Public Mindfulness:**

Social Awareness and Neighborhood Commitment:

Worldwide points of view on lion protection highlight the significance of social awareness and nearby commitment. Protection drives should regard assorted social convictions and practices to guarantee the achievement and manageability of endeavors. Inclusivity turns into a foundation of worldwide protection, perceiving the interconnectedness of human societies with the conservation of biodiversity.

Media and Innovation as Impetuses:

Public mindfulness expects a crucial job in worldwide lion preservation. Media and innovation act as impetuses, contacting a worldwide crowd with messages of preservation earnestness. Narratives, online entertainment crusades, and computer generated reality encounters upgrade public comprehension and motivate a feeling of obligation. The job of public mindfulness in pushing for protection arrangements and supporting drives becomes basic to the progress of worldwide preservation objectives.

Worldwide Coordinated effort Stages:

The worldwide point of view on lion preservation underlines global cooperation stages. Networks that unite specialists, associations, and state run administrations empower the sharing of information, assets, and best practices. By cultivating joint effort on a worldwide scale, the preservation local area intensifies its effect and makes a brought together front against the dangers looked by lions around the world.

8.2 The significance of the transition from enclosure to savanna for lion well-being

The change from nook to savanna addresses a stupendous change in the worldview of lion preservation, with significant ramifications for the prosperity of these lofty animals. Lions, once restricted to counterfeit nooks, end up very nearly recovering a similarity to their normal living space — the extensive savanna. This shift isn't just representative; it holds the way to opening physical, mental, and environmental advantages that can altogether upgrade the general prosperity of lions. In investigating this change, we dig into the meaning of furnishing lions with a savanna climate, remembering it as an extraordinary undertaking that lines up with the natural impulses and environmental necessities of these dominant hunters.

1. **Reconnecting with Nature:**
   Reclamation of Normal Ways of behaving:
   The change to a savanna climate offers lions the potential chance to take part in regular ways of behaving that were obliged in conventional nooks. The savanna, with its immense spaces, takes into consideration exercises like hunting, following, and mingling that are natural for a lion's lifestyle. The reclamation of these normal ways of behaving is key to their prosperity, advancing

actual wellbeing and mental excitement.

Upgraded Actual Activity:

The sweeping scenes of the savanna urge lions to take part in expanded active work. As opposed to the restricted space of walled in areas, where development might be confined, the savanna gives a climate helpful for running, climbing, and investigating. This improved actual activity is indispensable for keeping up with the solid strength, cardiovascular wellbeing, and readiness of lions.

2. **Mental Advancement:**

Feeling through Ecological Intricacy:

The savanna, with its assorted geography, vegetation, and natural life, presents a component of ecological intricacy that invigorates the mental and tactile resources of lions. The consistently evolving territory, the presence of regular impediments, and the valuable chance to collaborate with different improvements add to mental enhancement. This enhancement is critical for forestalling fatigue, diminishing pressure, and advancing mental prosperity.

Social Elements and Communication:

Lions are intrinsically friendly creatures, living in prides that cultivate complex social designs. Conventional walled in areas frequently restricted the social elements among lions, prompting possible pressure and conduct issues.

The change to the savanna takes into consideration a more regular articulation of social ways of behaving, including common hunting, prepping, and the foundation of orders inside prides. These connections add to the profound prosperity of lions.

3. **Natural Amicability:**

Reclamation of Environmental Equilibrium:

The savanna addresses a microcosm of natural equilibrium, with different species coinciding in a dynamic and interconnected snare of life. Lions, as dominant hunters, assume a vital part in directing prey populaces and keeping up with the soundness of environments. By changing lions to the savanna, traditionalists add to the rebuilding of natural equilibrium, guaranteeing that these dominant hunters satisfy their biological jobs.

Conservation of Regular Impulses:

Nooks frequently limit the statement of a lion's regular impulses, reducing their capacity to chase, investigate, and draw in with the climate. The savanna, as a more regular setting, jam and supports these senses. The demonstration of chasing after food, checking domains, and answering natural upgrades permits lions to reconnect with their intrinsic ways of behaving, cultivating a feeling of direction and satisfaction.

4. **Protection Suggestions:**

Advancement of Species-explicit Protection Objectives:

The progress from nook to savanna lines up with more extensive species-explicit protection objectives. As lions flourish in a climate that imitates their normal territory, they become stronger and versatile. This flexibility is significant for future renewed introduction endeavors, as lions brought up in a savanna climate are more ready to explore the difficulties of nature.

Commitment of Neighborhood People group:

The meaning of this progress stretches out past the prosperity of individual lions; it draws in neighborhood networks in the more extensive protection account. The presence of lions in a savanna climate can cultivate a feeling of satisfaction and possession among networks, underscoring the common obligation regarding the conservation of these dominant hunters. This people group commitment is vital for the drawn out progress of protection drives.

5. **Moral Contemplations:**

Arrangement with Moral Hostage The board:

The progress from nook to savanna lines up with advancing moral contemplations in hostage creature the executives. Conventional nooks, frequently reprimanded for confining regular ways of behaving, are step by step giving way to additional far reaching and naturalistic conditions. This shift mirrors a pledge to moral hostage the board that focuses on the prosperity and characteristic necessities of hostage creatures.

Upgraded Personal satisfaction:

From a moral point of view, giving lions a savanna climate adds to an upgraded personal satisfaction. The capacity to wander, investigate, and participate in normal ways of behaving encourages a feeling of opportunity that is essential to the prosperity of hostage creatures. Moral contemplations underline the significance of consistently assessing and working on hostage conditions to satisfy the developing guidelines of creature government assistance.

8.3 Call to action for continued efforts in improving lion welfare and conservation

The reverberations of a lion's thunder resonate through the savannas, filling in as a base source of inspiration for mankind to protect the fate of these notable animals. Regardless of critical steps in lion government assistance and preservation, our process is not even close to finished. This source of inspiration rallies us to maintain and enhance our endeavors, perceiving the pressing requirement for proceeded with devotion, development, and coordinated effort to guarantee the prosperity and protection of lions for a long time into the future.

1. **The Accomplishments and Difficulties:**
   Observing Achievements:
   Pondering the accomplishments in lion government assistance and protection brings a feeling of achievement. Effective renewed introduction programs, the change from nooks to additional regular habitats, and the commitment of nearby networks highlight the headway made. These achievements are demonstrations of the commitment of moderates, scientists, and networks working connected at the hip.
   Going up against Waiting Difficulties:
   In any case, the excursion isn't without challenges. Human-

natural life struggle continues, environment misfortune compromises biological systems, and criminal operations present critical dangers to lion populaces. Recognizing these difficulties is urgent to making informed systems that address the underlying drivers and encourage practical concurrence among people and lions.

2. **The Continuous Tasks and Drives:**
Preservation Through Coordinated effort:
Progressing tasks and drives show the force of coordinated effort. Preservation is an aggregate undertaking that rises above borders, and by pooling assets, information, and mastery, we can address complex difficulties all the more really. The soul of cooperation guarantees that preservation endeavors are dynamic, versatile, and sensitive to the advancing requirements of lions and their living spaces.

Economical Practices and Advancement:
The source of inspiration incorporates a promise to feasible practices and development. Green advances, moral hostage the executives, and progressions in observing and research add to the developing scene of lion preservation. By embracing development, we upgrade the prosperity of lions as well as prepare for a more practical and amicable connection among people and natural life.

Instruction and Promotion:
Instruction and promotion remain foundations of the source of inspiration. Engaging people group with information about lion preservation encourages a feeling of obligation and pride in protecting these dominant hunters. Public mindfulness crusades, school projects, and local area commitment drives enhance the source of inspiration, transforming people into advocates for lion government assistance and the protection of biodiversity.

3. **Examples Learned and Versatile Procedures:**
Considering Previous mishaps:
The source of inspiration urges us to consider previous oversights

and gain from them. Versatile techniques are brought into the world from a nuanced comprehension of the complex trap of elements impacting lion preservation. By recognizing stumbles, we prepare for versatile, proof based approaches that answer the unique difficulties looked by lions in the wild and in imprisonment.

Comprehensive Biological system The executives:

All encompassing environment the executives arises as a core value. The protection of lions is indistinguishable from the wellbeing of their biological systems. The source of inspiration underscores a comprehensive methodology that thinks about the interconnectedness of greenery, fauna, and networks. Safeguarding biodiversity and relieving the effect of environmental change become fundamental parts of an exhaustive protection technique.

Comprehensive Navigation:

Comprehensive dynamic cycles are fundamental for the outcome of the source of inspiration. Nearby people group, native information holders, analysts, and policymakers should team up in forming preservation arrangements. Inclusivity guarantees that drives are socially delicate, socially fair, and logically significant, encouraging a feeling of shared proprietorship and obligation.

4. **Future Ramifications and Looking Forward:**

Expecting Progress Achievement:

The source of inspiration expects the outcome of continuous progress endeavors. As lions change from bondage to additional indigenous habitats, the ramifications stretch out past individual prosperity. The triumphs and misfortunes become priceless illustrations that guide future undertakings. The source of inspiration empowers a forward-looking viewpoint, where the flexibility of lions fills in as motivation for versatile protection techniques.

Graphing a Course for Reasonable Preservation:

Looking forward includes graphing a course for reasonable

preservation. The source of inspiration perceives the significance of tending to all-encompassing difficulties, for example, environmental change, living space discontinuity, and the requirement for adjusted human-natural life concurrence. Supportable protection rehearses should be implanted in the texture of cultural qualities, strategies, and global collaboration.

5. **Worldwide Viewpoints and Public Mindfulness: Worldwide Coordinated effort for Lion Preservation:**

The source of inspiration expands all around the world, underscoring the interconnectedness of lion protection endeavors. Lions occupy assorted locales across Africa, each with its novel difficulties. The source of inspiration empowers worldwide coordinated effort stages that work with data sharing, asset assignment, and joint drives. Lions become representatives for worldwide participation, connecting social and topographical partitions.

Public Mindfulness as an Impetus:

Public mindfulness expects a focal job in the source of inspiration. Media, innovation, and instructive missions become impetuses for preparing a worldwide local area. The source of inspiration urges people to become educated advocates, impacting arrangements, supporting preservation drives monetarily, and advocating maintainable practices in their day to day routines. A groundswell of public help turns into an imposing power for change.

6. **Moral Contemplations and Mindful Stewardship:**

Moral Hostage The board as a Norm:

Moral contemplations highlight the source of inspiration, especially in the domain of hostage the board. The shift towards naturalistic conditions, moral rearing practices, and the progressively eliminating of obsolete presentation models mirrors a pledge to the prosperity of hostage lions. Moral hostage the executives turns into the norm by which we measure our obligation as stewards of these brilliant animals.

Dependable Stewardship of the Planet:
The source of inspiration stretches out past lions to include a more extensive obligation regarding the planet. As stewards of Earth, we are entrusted with protecting biodiversity, moderating environmental change, and cultivating a reasonable concurrence with the regular world. Dependable stewardship turns into a core value, encouraging us to proceed with caution, lessen environmental impressions, and champion strategies that focus on the prosperity of every living being.

www.ingramcontent.com/pod-product-compliance
Lightning Source LLC
Chambersburg PA
CBHW051831150726

47998CB00001B/381